AN

HISTORICAL SKETCH

OF

COLUMBIA COLLEGE,

IN THE

CITY OF NEW YORK,

1754–1876.

PRINTED FOR THE COLLEGE.
1876.

MACGOWAN & SLIPPER, Printers,
30 Beekman St., N. Y.

PREFACE.

This historical sketch of Columbia College and its associate Schools was prepared at the request of the National Bureau of Education in Washington. The history from the foundation of the college to the year 1845 is essentially that written by the former President, Dr. N. F. Moore, and printed in 1846. For the period from 1845 to 1869, the chief source of information was a continuation of Dr. Moore's history by Rev. Beverley R. Betts, Librarian of the College. The article on the School of Law was furnished by Professor T. W. Dwight, Warden of the School; that on the School of Mines was obtained from documents issued by the School, from the records, and from information furnished by the several Professors; that on the School of Medicine was taken mainly from the historical sketch of the College of Physicians and Surgeons, N. Y., which appeared in the general catalogue of that college published in 1866. The article on the College Library is the article on "Columbia College Library," by the late Librarian, W. A. Jones, Esq., published in the University Quarterly for January, 1871, as abridged and revised for this sketch by Professor Drisler; that on library of the School of Mines was prepared by Mr. John F. Meyer, Librarian and Registrar of the School. The article on Cabinets and Collections was compiled from inventories of the several departments in the hands of the Treasurer, and from information obtained of professors in charge. The Financial Statement is from the last annual report of the Board of Trustees to the Regents of the University of the State of New York, for the year ending Sept. 30, 1875.

Such parts of the Sketch as have not been accounted for in the above statement, have for their authority documents issued by the college and its several schools, and the resolutions of the Board of Trustees.

In an Appendix will be found the original charter of the college and the Acts of the Legislature of the State of New York relating to the college.

J. H. VAN AMRINGE.

COLUMBIA COLLEGE, N. Y., July, 1876.

NOTE.

THE statement on pages 49, 50, that the annuity of £750, granted by the State for five years, was discontinued on the expiration of that period, is a mistake. Before the expiration of the period named in the first Act, a second Act was passed continuing the annuity for a further term of two years.

On page 73, in mentioning the division of certain chairs, it should be noted that, at the same time, the chair of the Greek and Latin Languages was divided into two, viz.: that of the Greek Language and Literature, which Professor Anthon retained, and that of the Latin Language and Literature, to which adjunct Professor Drisler was promoted.

To the statement on page 80 that the chair of Constitutional History and Public Law has not been filled since the death of Dr. Lieber, should be added that, in the spring of 1876, the chair of History, Political Science, and International Law was created, and Professor John W. Burgess, A. M., elected to fill it. A similar statement should be added in the account of the Law School on page 84.

CONTENTS.

COLUMBIA COLLEGE.

AT what period the design of establishing a college in New York was first seriously entertained does not appear. The earliest intimation that has been discovered of any such design "is contained in the records of Trinity Church. From them it appears that as early as the year 1703, the Rector and Wardens were directed to wait upon Lord Cornbury, the Governor, to know what part of the *King's Farme*, then vested in Trinity Church, had been intended for the college which he designed to have built."—*Address delivered before the Alumni of Col. Coll. by C. C. Moore.*

Some such plan was thought of again, it seems, in 1729, during Berkeley's residence in this country; and when disappointed as regarded Bermuda, he sought to transfer the establishment which had been intended for that island to "some place on the American Continent, which would probably have been New York."—*Chandler's Life of Johnson.*

But Berkeley's benevolent design having altogether failed, we find no mention of this subject until near twenty years afterwards, when several laws of the Colony were passed for raising moneys by way of lottery, towards the founding of a college therein; and Bishop Berkeley, in a letter of August 23d, 1749, to Dr. Johnson, who resided then at Hartford, in Connecticut, says: "For the rest, I am glad to find a spirit toward learning prevails in those parts, particularly New York, where you say a college is projected, which has my best wishes.'

The earliest of the laws just now alluded to, received the Governor's assent on the 6th of December, 1746, nnd was entitled "An act for raising the sum of two thousand two hundred and fifty pounds, by a public lottery for this colony, for the encouragement of learning, and towards the founding a college within the same."

Other similar acts followed, and in November, 1751, the moneys raised by means of them, amounting then to £3,443 18*s.* 0*d.*, were vested in trustees. Of these trustees, ten in number, two belonged to the Dutch Reformed Church, one was a Presbyterian, but seven were members of the Church of England, and some of these seven were also vestrymen of Trinity Church. These circumstances—the known sentiments of this large majority of the trustees—their well understood, and very natural desire, that the proposed college should be connected with their church—might sufficiently account for the offer made to them by Trinity Church, not long after their appointment, "of any reasonable quantity of the Church farm, (which was not let out) for erecting, and use of a college;" from what has been already stated, however, respecting the first mention of a college in the province—from the inquiry addressed by Trinity Church to Lord Cornbury, in 1703—it may not unreasonably be inferred, that the then recent grant of the King's Farm to that corporation, had been made with a view to the advancement of learning as well as of religion; that some condition to that effect had been at least implied, on occasion of that grant.

If such were the case, the present offer from the church was but the carrying out, after a lapse of fifty years, of this original design.

As regards the offer now made to the Trustees, it seems highly probable that some such conditions as we find afterwards expressed in the conveyance from the Church to the College, when actually made, were, from the first, in contemplation of the parties, and understood between them; but neither in the proposal from the Church, on the 8th of April, 1752, nor in the report made thereof by the Trustees to the Assembly, more than two years afterwards, is there mention of any conditions whatever. The natural inference, however, which has been suggested, as to their existence, and the jealous apprehensions entertained of any, the smallest, approach to a church-establishment within the province, caused violent opposition to the plan, as soon as it became known, of obtaining a royal charter for the college.

This opposition, and the angry controversy to which it gave rise, delayed the granting of the charter of King's College, which was finally obtained on October 31st, 1754.

Previously, however, to the granting of the charter, the friends of the proposed College had not been inactive. On the 22d of November, 1753, the Trustees, previously designated, determined to invite the Rev. Dr. Samuel Johnson, of Stratford, to accept the presidency of the intended college, with a salary of £250, and Mr. Chauncey Whittlesey, of New Haven, as his assistant, with a salary of £200. They were sensible, they said, that the salary proposed for Dr. Johnson (though as much as they were able to offer) was inadequate to his merit; but they expressed their belief, that the vestry of Trinity Church would readily agree to make a sufficient addition thereto; and such of the Trustees as were also vestrymen, were desired to recommend this measure to the vestry. And that appears to have been done accordingly; for on the 7th of January, 1754, the Trustees informed Dr. Johnson by letter, that the vestry of Trinity Church had agreed to call him as an assistant minister. In his answer, dated February 11th, 1754, he neither accepts nor rejects the proposal, but requires further time to consider of the matter.

He came to New York in the month of April following, and entered upon the duties of the presidency about three months afterwards.

At a meeting of the Trustees on the 16th of May, 1754, about a month after Dr. Johnson's removal to the city, was read a draft of the proposed charter, against which a formal protest was offered. The application for the charter was proceeded with, in spite of opposition; and in anticipation of the more formal establishment of their College, the Trustees gave public notice of an examination of candidates for admission, to be held during the first week of the following July, and on the 17th of that month, Dr. Johnson began, in the vestry-room of the school-house belonging to Trinity Church, his instruction of the eight students who were admitted at this first examination. These were, Samuel Verplanck, Rudolph Ritzema, Philip Van Cortlandt, Robert Bayard, Samuel Provoost, Thomas Marston, Henry Cruger, and Joshua Bloomer; and whoever has an old acquaintance with the city of New York will recognize among them several familiar and respected names.

The royal charter constituting King's College passed the seals, as was previously mentioned, on the 31st of October, 1754; but the organization of the college under it cannot be considered as having taken place before the 7th of May, 1755, when, at a meeting of above twenty of the gentlemen named in it as Governors, Mr. Goldsbrow Banyar, Deputy Secretary of the province, attending with the charter, the Lieutenant Governor, James De Lancey, after a suitable address, delivered it to the gentlemen present, and Mr. Horsmanden, one of the Judges of the Supreme Court, qualified them as Governors by administering the oaths by law required to be taken. After which Mr. Chambers, who presided at this meeting, in a reply to the Lieutenant Governor, on behalf of the Governors of the college, expressed most grateful acknowledgments of the honor he had been pleased to confer on them in their appointment, and hoped their conduct, as Governors of that corporation, would always merit the continuance of his honor's protection, favor and countenance, and convince the world that they had nothing more at heart than to promote the glory of God, the true Protestant religion, and a generous education of their youth in the liberal arts and sciences.

We may gather whence arose this delay of above six months, between the date and the delivery of the charter, from a letter written by Dr. Johnson to Bishop Sherlock, on the very day of such delivery, in which he says, "I humbly thank your Lordship for the most kind regard you express towards me, in view of my undertaking the care of this young college, which I hope will live in spite of the most virulent opposition it meets with. The charter at last passed the seals in October, while I was returned into the country. But the clamour was so great, that there were some alterations in the draught after I went away, for which I was very sorry, and particularly that the Bishop of London was left out from being one of the Governors." "I was in great doubt whether to *accept* the presidency: but as I saw that it would come to nothing if I did *not*, I at length returned and accepted the charge. Mr. Beach has concluded to succeed me at Stratford; so I am settled here in New York, being also lecturer in Trinity Church."

The charter, when delivered, named as governors of the College, the Archbishop of Canterbury, and the first Lord Commissioner for trade and plantations, who were empowered to act by proxy, the Lieutenant Governor and Commander-in-chief of the Province of New York, the eldest Councillor of the Province, the Judges of the Supreme Court of Judicature of the Province, the Secretary, the Attorney General, the Speaker of the General Assembly, and the Treasurer of the Province, the Mayor of the City of New York, the Rector of Trinity Church, the Senior Minister of the Reformed Protestant Dutch Church, the Ministers of the Ancient Lutheran Church, of the French Church, and of the Presbyterian Congregation in the City of New York, and the President of the college—all these *ex officio*, and together with them four and twenty of the principal gentlemen of the city, who were: Archibald Kennedy, Joseph Murray, Josiah Martin, Paul Richard, Henry Cruger, William Walton, John Watts, Henry Beekman, Philip Ver Planck, Frederick Philipse, Joseph Robinson, John Cruger, Oliver De Lancey, James Livingston, Esqrs,, Benjamin Nicoll, William Livingston, Joseph Read, Nathaniel Marston, Joseph Haynes, John Livingston, Abraham Lodge, David Clarkson, Leonard Lispenard, and James De Lancey, the younger, Gentlemen.

The college being now incorporated, and capable of holding the land previously destined for it by Trinity Church, and mentioned in its charter, at the next meeting of the governors, on the 13th of May, 1755, the corporation of Trinity Church delivered to them deeds of conveyance of a piece of land described therein as situate on the west side of the Broadway, in the west ward of the City of New York, fronting easterly to Church-street, between Barclay-street and Murray-street, four hundred and forty feet, and thence running westerly along Barclay-street and Murray-street to the North River.

The conditions of this gift to the college—conditions which, being inserted in its charter also, afforded pretext for the furious opposition it encountered—were, that its President for ever, for the time being, should be a member of and in communion with the Church of England, as by law established; and that the morning and evening service in the college should be the liturgy of the said church, or such a collection of prayers out of that liturgy, together with a collect peculiar for the college, as should be approved by its president and governors.

All who have any acquaintance with our college, or its history, will know how wholly unfounded has proved the inference from those conditions, that towards students who happened to belong to the communion of which its president was required to be, the slightest preference or favor would on that account be shown.

The charter, indeed, expressly denied to the college the power of making any laws or regulations tending " to exclude any person of any religious denomination whatever, from equal liberty and advantage of education, or from any of the degrees, liberties, privileges, benefits, and immunities of said College, on account of his particular tenets in matters of religion."

To show how little the conditions, which exposed the college to so much obloquy, were considered at the time, by dispassionate men, as stamping the institution with any bigoted or exclusive character, it may suffice to state the very first act and proceeding of its Governors.

At their first meeting on the 7th of May, 1755, after the acceptance of the charter, the speech of the Lieutenant Governor, and the reply of Mr. Chambers, the Rev. Mr. Ritzema, senior minister of the Reformed Protestant Dutch Church, among other things addressed by him to the Lieutenant Governor, remarked that he was sorry to have observed the differences and animosities in the Province touching several restrictions in the charter. He expressed his hope that some means might be fallen upon to heal them ; and his belief that it would conduce greatly to that end if his Honour would be pleased to grant, either by addition to the charter, or in such other manner as should be thought most proper, that there should be established in the college a professor of divinity, for the education of such of the youth of their church as might be intended for the ministry, with a suitable allowance of salary, and to be chosen by the consistory of that church for the time being. The Lieutenant Governor, in reply, expressed his approval of Mr. Ritzema's suggestion, and his willingness to grant any application in accordance with it that the Governors might address to him. The Governors at once, unanimously, adopted Mr. Ritzema's proposal, and appointed a committee to prepare their petition accordingly; which being reported at their next meeting and approved, the same committee was directed to present it, and at the meeting after, on the 3d of June, Mr. Banyar, Deputy Secretary of the Province, delivered to the Governors his Majesty's additional charter, making provision for the establishment of a professor in divinity, according to the doctrine, discipline, aud worship established by the National Synod of Dort.

At a meeting on the 3d of June, 1755, was adopted the device prepared by Dr. Johnson for the seal of King's College, and which continues to be that of Columbia College, with only the necessary alteration of its name. The description given of this device, which is here inserted, deserves notice as showing how deservedly pre-eminent a place religion held in education, according to the ideas of those who laid the foundations of our discipline.*

(This description is copied literally from the minutes.)

"THE DEVICE OF THE COLLEGE SEAL.—The College is represented by a Lady sitting in a Throne or Chair of State, with Severall Children at her knees to represent the Pupils, with I Peter, II., 1, 2, 7 v., under them to express the Temper with which they should apply Themselves to seek for True Wisdom. The words are, Wherefore laying aside all Malice and all Guile, and Hypocrisies and Envies and Evil Speakings, as New-born Babes desire the Sincere Milk of the Word that ye may grow thereby, &c. One of them She takes by the hand with her left hand expressing her benevolent design of Conducting them to true Wisdom and Virtue. To which purpose She holds open to them a Book in her right hand in which is [in] Greek letters ΛΌΓΙΑ ΖΩ͂ΝΤΑ, the living or lively Oracles, which is the Epithet that St. Stephen gives to the Holy Scriptures—Acts 7 : 38. Out of her Mouth over her left Shoulder,goes a Label with these words in Hebrew Letters ORI-EL—God is my Light; alluding to Ps. 27 : 1, expressing her Acknowledgment of God the Father of Lights, as the Fountain of all that Light, both Natural and Revealed with which She proposes to inlighten or instruct her Children or Pupils; whereof the Sun rising under the Label is the Emblem or Hieroglyphic, alluding to that expression Mal. IV., 2.

* It was, indeed, with a view chiefly to religion that all the earlier literary institutions of our country were established. This was true especially of Harvard, William and Mary, Yale, and Princeton colleges, as is shown by the Rev. Dr. Alva Woods, in his Valedictory Address to the University of Alabama, p. 34.

The Sun of Righteousness arising with healing in his Wings. Over her head is Jehovah in a Glory, the Beams coming triangularly to a Point near her head, with these words around her for her Motto, IN LUMINE TUO VIDEBIMUS LUMEN—*In thy light shall we see light.*—Psal. 36: 9. On the Edge around are engraved in Capitals, SIGILLUM COLLEGII REG. NOV. EBOR. IN AMERICA—*The Seal of King's College at New York in America.*"

In the summer of 1756, the Governors of the Institution, having provided for other exigencies of the College, proceeded to erect a building for its accommodation. The plan for this having, in compliment to Sir Charles Hardy, been submitted to him, and having received his approbation, was adopted by the Governors on the 13th of July, 1756; and on the 23d of the following month the first stone was laid by Sir Charles Hardy, and the President addressed the Governors of the College, Sir Charles Hardy, and the Lieutenant Governor, Mr. De Lancey, in a brief Latin speech, congratulating them on this happy event, which had succeeded almost beyond expectation "Per varios casus et tot discrimina rerum."

The inscription on this first stone, which was beneath the south-east corner of the central or older portion of the college building in College Place, was as follows:—

Hujus Collegii, Regalis dicti, Regio
Diplomate constituti in Honorem
Dei O. M. atq: in Ecclesiæ Reiq: Publicæ
Emolumentum, primum hunc lapidem
posuit Vir præcellentissimus, Carolus
Hardy, Eques Auratus, hujus Provinciæ
Præfectus dignissimus. Aug^{ti}. die 23°.
An. Dom. MDCCLVI.

During the year 1755, a second class having been admitted into college, an additional instructor became indispensable, and Mr. Wm. Johnson, A.M., a young gentleman who had received his education at Yale College, was appointed to the place which had been originally offered to Mr. Whittlesey. Mr. Johnson, after holding his office for about a year, went to England to take orders, and Mr. Leonard Cutting, of Pembroke Hall, Cambridge, a thorough-bred classical scholar, was in 1756 appointed in his stead.

In November of the following year, 1757, Dr. Johnson was driven from New York by the small-pox, and remained in the adjacent county of Westchester for above a year.

Although when Dr. Johnson retired from the city there were not above thirty students altogether in the then three classes, yet, Mr. Cutting being unequal to the care of all, the Governors, on the 8th of November, 1757, appointed Mr. Treadwell a young gentleman of excellent character, educated at Harvard College, and recommended by Professor Winthrop as eminently qualified for the station, to be professor of Mathematics and Natural Philosophy; and to aid his instructions an apparatus of instruments for teaching Experimental Philosophy was imported from Europe. It was made a part of Mr. Treadwell's duty to teach also the Latin and Greek languages to the two younger classes.

Dr. Johnson returned to the city, and to his more immediate care of the college, in March, 1758; and on the 21st of June following was held the first commencement; at which the degree of Bachelor of Arts was conferred on eight students, five of whom were of the number of those admitted in 1754—the other three had been educated either in Philadelphia or at Princeton. At this same commencement twelve gentlemen, who had been elsewhere educated, were created Masters of Arts, or, holding that degree already from some other institution, were admitted *ad eundem*.

The year following, there was no public commencement; but the degree of Bachelor of Arts was conferred on two candidates, one of whom had been educated at Princeton, and the other was, out of six admitted in 1755, the only one who had completed his four years of study. The remarks made in the Matricula of the College respecting those who entered the Freshman Class together with him are, of one, that he "in his third year went to Philadelphia College;" of another, that "about the middle of his second year he went into the army;" of another, that he "after three years went to merchandise;" of the fourth, that "after about two years he went to privateering;" and of the fifth, that he "after three years went to nothing." Similar brief remarks are found throughout the Matricula of King's College, on those who left it before the completion of their course. One "left College in his second year, having behaved very indifferently." Another went away in his third year, "and was not much regretted." And of another, again, we find "the loss regretted."

In October of this year, 1759, dread of the small-pox again drove Dr. Johnson out of town, and during his absence, which lasted until the month of May following, the duties of the College were, for a time, divided between Mr. Cutting and Professor Treadwell; but the declining health of the latter, and his death in 1760, made it necessary to seek some one qualified to take his place; and such an one, it seems, was not at that period easily found. During the interval of about eighteen months between the death of Professor Treadwell and the appointment of his successor, Mr. Samuel Giles was for a time employed as an instructor in Mathematics.

In February, 1760, a committee was appointed to write to the Archbishop of Canterbury, and such other persons as they might think fit, to procure two proper persons "to assist the President in carrying on the education and instruction of the youth of the College."

This resolution of the Governors, and Dr. Johnson's own desire to provide a successor to himself—some one on whom he might, within a few years at farthest, devolve the duties of the presidency—gave occasion for several letters on both sides between him and Archbishop Secker, who seems to have taken much pains, though for a long time without success, to obtain such a person as the College required.

Meantime the College building had been so far completed that the officers and students began to lodge and mess there in May, 1760; and on the 26th of the following month the procession proceeded thence to St. George's Chapel to hold the third annual commencement. On this occasion the President, in a Latin speech, congratulated the Governors assembled for the first time in the College Hall.

The building thus completed was that older portion of the old college edifice in College Place which was contained between the wings. It constituted one-third part of the original design, and in the minutes of the Governors is repeatedly styled *the north side of the College.* An English traveller in the province at that period, the Rev. Dr. Burnaby, remarks, " The college when finished will be exceedingly handsome. It is to be built on three sides of a quadrangle fronting Hudson's or North River, and will be the most beautifully situated of any college, I believe, in the world. At present only one wing is finished, which is of stone, and consists of twenty-four sets of apartments, each having a large sitting room with a study and bedchamber." The same writer speaks of the president as "a very worthy and learned man, but rather too far advanced in life to have the direction of so young an institution."

In November, 1761, the place of Mr. Treadwell was at length filled by the appointment of Mr. Robert Harpur, a gentleman educated at Glasgow, as professor of Mathematics and Natural Philosophy. It was some time longer, however, before Archbishop Secker's inquiries succeeded in finding any one fitted to aid Dr. Johnson in discharging the duties of his office, and after a while to succeed him in it. The person at length selected for this purpose was the Rev. Myles Cooper,

A. M., a Fellow of Queen's College, Oxford, who came out in the autumn of 1762. From the Archbishop, who had on several previous occasions mentioned him, he brought a letter dated Aug. 18th, 1762, which begins, "Good Dr. Johnson. The bearer is Mr. Cooper. God grant he may prove a proper man, and useful among you." In November following, Mr. Cooper was appointed Fellow of the college, Professor of Moral Philosophy, and to assist the President in his instruction and government. This instruction, given by the President, had, since the regular organization of the college, been confined to Greek, Logic, Metaphysics, and Ethics.

Archbishop Secker continued to testify a lively interest in Mr. Cooper's success, and the welfare of the college, mentioning him repeatedly in subsequent letters; and on the 30th of March, 1763, he writes, in reference to Dr. Johnson's (then, as he thought, only proposed) resignation, "I assure you I will do nothing to retard your retirement, beyond expressing my wishes that you would be so kind to your college, and to Mr. Cooper, as to give him competent time for becoming, and showing himself in some degree proper to succeed you." But Dr. Johnson had already, on the 1st of March, resigned his office, and on the 12th of April following, Mr. Cooper, upon whom his duties had meantime devolved, was elected to supply his place. Dr. Johnson returned to Stratford, where, in the midst of his son's family, surrounded by numerous old friends, he passed the quiet remainder of his days.

At the same meeting at which Dr. Johnson's resignation was announced, a plan was adopted for the establishment of a grammar school in connection with the college, and this was opened not long afterwards under the charge of Mr. Matthew Cushing, of Charlestown, Massachusetts. A librarian also was appointed, and a new body of laws, better adapted, as was thought, to the actual condition of the college, received the assent of the Governors, and on the following day was announced in their presence in the College Hall. Among the changes which it introduced was a great enlargement of the scheme of studies in the classical department.

When Dr. Johnson retired from the college he left there four and twenty students; a very inconsiderable number, it is true, but equivalent, nevertheless, to nine hundred at the present day, if proportionate regard be had to the population of the city at that period and now. Of these twenty-four, and the thirteen admitted during the two following years, only twenty-eight in all completed their college course, and were graduated; but we find among them a very unusual proportion of distinguished men. The biographer of one of them, Peter Van Schaack, after mentioning that he entered the Freshman class in 1762, remarks, "This was an eventful era in his life. It was here that he formed an interesting and valuable acquaintance with John Jay, Egbert Benson, Richard Harison, Gouverneur Morris, Robert R. Livingston, and many other illustrious men, whose enviable reputations now constitute the richest property of their country."

The first commencement at which Mr. Cooper presided, was held in St. George's Chapel, on the 17th of May, 1763, five weeks after his appointment, when two students were admitted to the degree of Bachelor, and seven alumni of the college to that of Master of Arts.

The commencement of the following year also was held at St. George's Chapel; but all the commencements of King's College subsequent to that were in Trinity Church, except those of 1767 and 1768, which were at St. Paul's Chapel. Respecting that of 1765, in Trinity Church, we find mentioned, as if it were a novelty, that three anthems, and several other pieces of music were performed; and so of the following commencement, also, it is stated that "the exercises were intermixed with music."

For near six months after Mr. Cooper's appointment to the presidency, he had the aid of both Mr. Cutting and Mr. Harpur, as instructors in the college; but on the resignation of the former in October, 1763, he greatly needed the assistance of some other teacher. Negotiations were entered into with Mr. Richardson and other gentlemen of Oxford, and efforts were made in other quarters, but for a long time in vain, to find some suitable person to fill Mr. Cutting's place. At length, on the 24th of October, 1765, Dr. Clossy, a gentleman educated at Trinity College, Dublin, and who, before his emigration to America, had attained a high standing in his profession, by the publication of an able work on Morbid Anatomy, was appointed tutor, with a salary of £144, and a further salary of £36 was assigned to him as Professor of Natural Philosophy; Professor Harpur, to whom this subject had previously belonged, teaching thenceforth only Mathematics.

The affairs of the college seem to have gone on prosperously now for several years. The classes were taught by Mr. Cooper, Mr. Harpur, and Dr. Clossy, and under such able instructors possessed advantages which, perhaps, no seminary of so young a standing in this country had enjoyed.

On the 26th of February, 1767, a committee previously appointed to petition Sir Henry Moore,

Governor of the province, for a grant of land, made report that they had obtained one of 24,000 acres. The same committee was thereupon empowered to view the lands, and, if it was thought fit, to have them surveyed. From subsequent proceedings of the Governors, in relation to these lands, on the 20th of March, 1770, when measures for their more speedy settlement were adopted, it appears that they were situate in the new county of Gloucester, in the province of New-York; that they were not only erected into a township, with the usual privileges, but to the great advantage, as was hoped, of the college, were constituted to become the county town.

All these anticipations, however, were to be disappointed. Unluckily for the college, its township was comprehended within that tract of country which, after being in dispute for six and twenty years between New York and New Hampshire, or settlers claiming under grants from her, was erected into the new State of Vermont, and all grants of lands lying within its limits, made by New York, were, in consideration of thirty thousand dollars, which it paid to New York, declared null and void.

This treaty, which the State of New York, from weighty considerations of public policy, rather than for the paltry sum of money paid, found it expedient to make, surrendered a property belonging to the college, which would at this day have been of immense value, and in so doing, may be regarded as having given to the college a claim for retribution, which all that the State has since done for it does not fully satisfy.

In February, 1767, Mr. Harpur, the professor of Mathematics, resigned his office, nor does it appear that any person was appointed in his place.

The Grammar School, established in 1763, seems not to have succeeded as was hoped. In August, 1767, it was found that the college had sunk by it about £370. Some reforms were therefore made, and its expenses were reduced by dispensing with one of the teachers until then employed. At the same time the Governors took an important step towards advancing the usefulness and reputation of the college, by their adoption of a scheme proposed by Dr. Clossy, in connection with Drs. Middleton, Jones, Smith, Bard, and Tennent, for the institution of a Medical School within the college.

The Governors having considered the plan submitted by these gentlemen, and their offer to give courses of lectures during the winter, each on some branch of his profession, expressed a high confidence in their merit, learning, and abilities, with a due sense of their generous and disinterested proposals, and unanimously appointed them to be professors—Samuel Clossy, M. D., of Anatomy; Peter Middleton, M. D., of Pathology and Physiology; John Jones, M. D., of Surgery; James Smith, M. D., of Chemistry and Materia Medica; Samuel Bard, M. D., of the Theory and Practice of Medicine; John V. B. Tennent, M. D., of Midwifery.

Three of these professors, the Doctors Middleton, Jones, and Bard, were shortly after this the most active promoters of that noble charity, the New York Hospital, and it appears from a medical discourse delivered by Dr. Middleton, at the college, on the 3d of November, 1769, that the first suggestion relative to the establishment of a hospital in New York was made by Dr. Bard. "The necessity and usefulness of a public infirmary," says Dr. Middleton, "has been so warmly and pathetically set forth, in a discourse delivered by Dr. Samuel Bard, at the College Commencement in May last, that his Excellency Sir Henry Moore immediately set on foot a subscription for that purpose, to which himself and most of the gentlemen present liberally contributed."—*Account of the N. Y. Hospital, p.* 63. *Historical Sketch of the Coll. of Phys. and Surgeons, p.* 7.

For several years after the organization of the

Faculty of Medicine, we find little of importance in the minutes of the Governors, besides what has been already noticed; nor is there any thing, as regards the college, derived from other quarters that deserves particular remark. The institution seems to have been advancing steadily in a prosperous and quiet course, except in so far as the daily increasing political excitement of the times may have disturbed it.

Among papers left in this country by Dr. Cooper (for so he may henceforth be styled, as he received in 1768, both from the University of Oxford, and from the Governors of King's College, the degree of LL.D.) there is one containing an account of King's College, which is ascribed to him. This account must have been written, not only after the establishment of the Medical School, but since Natural Law is mentioned in it as among the subjects taught, and there was no professor of that previous to 1773, it is probably to be assigned to some date not long after that.

This paper, after mentioning the manner in which the college was founded, and some leading provisions of its charter, then goes on to state that "Since the passing of the charter the Institution hath received great emolument by grants from his most gracious majesty King George the Third, and by liberal contributions from many of the nobility and gentry in the parent country; from the Society for the Propagation of the Gospel in Foreign Parts, and from several public-spirited gentlemen in America and elsewhere. By means of these and other benefactions, the Governors of the College have been enabled to extend their plan of education almost as diffusely as any college in Europe; herein being taught by proper Masters and Professors, who are chosen by the Governors and President, Divinity, Natural Law, Physic, Logic, Ethics, Metaphysics, Mathematics, Natural Philosophy, Astronomy, Geography, History, Chronology, Rhetoric, Hebrew, Greek, Latin, Modern Languages, the Belles Lettres, and whatever else of literature may tend to accomplish the pupils as scholars and gentlemen.

"To the College is also annexed a Grammar School for the due preparation of those who propose to complete their education with the arts and sciences.

"All students but those in Medicine, are obliged to lodge and diet in the College, unless they are particularly exempted by the Governors or President; and the edifice is surrounded by an high fence, which also encloses a large court and garden, and a porter constantly attends at the front gate, which is closed at ten o'clock each evening in summer and nine in winter; after which hours the names of all that come in are delivered weekly to the President.

"The College is situated on a dry, gravelly soil, about one hundred and fifty yards from the bank of the Hudson river, which it overlooks; commanding, from the eminence on which it stands, a most extensive and beautiful prospect of the opposite shore and country of New Jersey, the City and Island of New York, Long Island, Staten Island, New York Bay with its Islands, the Narrows, forming the mouth of the harbor, etc., etc.; and being totally unencumbered by any adjacent buildings, and admitting the purest circulation of air from the river, and every other quarter, has the benefit of as agreeable and healthy a situation as can possibly be conceived.

"Visitations by the Governors are quarterly; at which times, premiums of books, silver medals, etc., are adjudged to the most deserving.

"This Seminary hath already produced a number of gentlemen who do great honor to their professions, the place of their education, and themselves, in Divinity, Law, Medicine, etc., etc., in this and various other colonies, both on the American continent and West India Islands; and the College is annually increasing as well in students as reputation."

The Rev. John Vardill, A. M., appointed in

1773 Professor of Natural Law, and soon after of History and Languages also, was an alumnus of King's College, and the first one who was ever appointed to any office therein—a pupil of Dr. Cooper, he seems to have agreed with him entirely in politics. He must have left this country very soon after his appointment, if, indeed, he were not absent when it was made, for the writer of a letter from London, in the beginning of 1775, speaks of him as "Parson Vardill, a native of New York, who has been here a twelvemonth, a ministerial writer under the signature of *Coriolanus*, lately appointed King's Professor in the College of New York, with a salary of £200 sterling."

Dr. Cooper may have thought himself in duty bound to take an active part in the fierce strife of tongues and pens which, towards the close of his presidency, exercised the utmost powers of all who imagined they could use those weapons with effect. He of course "took the side of the British government, and distinguished himself in the political controversies of the day against Smith, Livingston and other literary champions of the whig party. In one of these skirmishes, he is said to have been met and worsted by an anonymous antagonist, whom he soon after discovered in the person of one of his own pupils, Alexander Hamilton, then a student in one of the younger classes.

It would be injustice to the memory of Dr. Cooper not to add, that far from betraying anything like mortification or resentment, he uniformly treated his youthful antagonist with good humor and even respect.—*Analectic Mag.*, *v.* 14, *p.* 96.

It may justly be regarded as a proof of the influence which liberal studies exercise upon the minds of youth, in awakening a love of liberty—a spirit intolerant of tyranny, injustice, and oppression—that, notwithstanding the political principles of those who administered the government of King's College, and especially of Dr. Cooper; and although the talents and popularity of the President might seem likely to recommend his opinions to his pupils, yet a large proportion of them were so far from adopting his tory principles, as to be among the foremost champions of liberty, in the cabinet and the field. "There were early found Jay and Livingston, Morris and Benson, Van Cortlandt and Rutgers, and Troup and Hamilton."—*Verplanck's Address, delivered before the Philolexian and Peithologian Societies of Col. Coll. p.* 13.

The name of Hamilton (whom the College has always insisted on reckoning as one of her alumni), stands conspicuous among those of students matriculated in 1774. Had the circumstances of the college and those eventful times allowed him to complete his academic course, it would, no doubt, considering his ardor and activity of mind, have been a brilliant one even within the college walls; but the voice of his country called him to a higher and more extended sphere of action. Abandoning the studious retirement of academic shades, to take part in the struggles of the battle-field, or the deliberations of the cabinet, he has made his name the property of the historian, and the theme of a loftier praise than any that these pages are able to award.

The boldness with which Dr. Cooper maintained, in his writings and his conversation, principles and sentiments highly offensive to a most numerous party, at a time of great popular excitement, at length so roused the indignation of his political opponents, that on the night of May 10th, 1775, his lodgings in the college were forcibly entered by a mob, to the fury of which, had he been found there, he would probably have fallen a victim. A few days previous, had been published a letter, dated Philadelphia, April 25, 1775, addressed to Dr. Cooper and four other obnoxious gentlemen of this city, ascribing to them, and to their assurances of the defection of New York, all the hostile proceedings of England—the blood of their fellow-subjects who had fallen in Massachusetts—towns in flames—a desolated country—butchered fathers, weeping widows and children, with all the horrors of a civil war. They are denounced as *parricides*, and told that the *Americans*, reduced to desperation, will no longer satisfy their resentment with the execution of villains in effigy; and the letter concludes:

"Fly for your lives, or anticipate your doom by becoming your own executioners.—THREE MILLIONS."—*Amer. Archives, 4th Series, vol. 2. col.* 389.

If those of the *three millions* who sought Dr. Cooper on this occasion, were animated by the wrathful spirit which breathes through this epistle, we may easily imagine the treatment he would have received from them. But their design was frustrated by one of his former pupils, who, preceding the throng of several hundred men, admonished him of his danger just in time to save him. He escaped, only half-dressed, over the college fence; reached the shore of the Hudson, and wandered along the river bank till near morning, when he found shelter in the house of his friend Mr. Stuyvesant, where he remained for that day, and during the night following took refuge on board the Kingfisher, Captain James Montagu, an English ship of war at anchor in the harbor, in which soon afterwards he sailed for England.

On the 16th of May, or six days after this narrow escape of the President, the Rev. Benjamin

Moore, an alumnus of the college, who a few months previous had returned from England in holy orders, was appointed by the Governors *Præses pro tempore;* it being supposed that Dr. Cooper might, which he never did, return.

In consequence of Dr. Cooper's absence there was no public commencement held this year; but the degree of Bachelor of Arts was conferred on seven students, and that of Master of Arts on two alumni of the college; and eight students were admitted.

On the 6th of April, in the following year, 1776, the Treasurer of the College received from the *Committee of Safety* a message, desiring the Governors to prepare the College within six days, for the reception of troops. The students were in consequence dispersed, the library and apparatus were deposited in the City Hall, or elsewhere, and the college edifice was converted into a military hospital. *Almost all the apparatus, and a large* proportion of the books belonging to the college, were wholly lost to it in consequence of this removal; and of the books recovered, six or seven hundred volumes were so, only after about thirty years, when they were found, with as many belonging to the N. Y. Society Library, and some belonging to Trinity Church, in a room in St. Paul's Chapel, where, it seemed, no one but the sexton had been aware of their existence, and neither he nor anybody else could tell how they had arrived here.

Previous to this dispersion of the college library, it contained, besides books purchased by the Governors and those bequeathed by Dr. Bristowe and by Mr. Murray, many valuable works given by the Earl of Bute and other individuals, and from the University of Oxford, a copy of every work printed at the University Press.

This forcible seizure of the college building, for as such, in fact, we may regard it, was perhaps suggested by the same feeling of political animosity that had been manifested with such violence in the attempt to seize on Dr. Cooper's person. The Committee of Safety, when they aimed this blow at an obnoxious institution, which they looked upon as a mere hot-bed of Toryism, were little aware of the fruits their country was about to reap from plants that had been reared in it.

An eminent jurist has remarked "that until the foundation of King's college, little more than twenty years before the Declaration of Independence, there were no seminaries within the colony, in which any other than a very indifferent education could be procured. The influence of that institution on the literary character of the State was truly wonderful; for though the whole number of students educated in the college prior to 1775 was but one hundred, many of them attained to great distinction in their respective professions and in public life. In reference to them and to their Alma Mater, the language of the Roman poet would scarcely be too strong."

> "Felix prole virum —— ——
> Læta deum partu, centum complexa nepotes,
> Omnes cœlicolas, omnes supera alta tenentes."

As a specimen of the elder born of this "Titanian progeny," our author names "Robert R. Livingston, Gouverneur Morris and John Jay, each distinguished, alike by his genius and erudition, and all illustrious in the annals of their country, for their talents as writers and their services as statesmen."—*Benj. F. Butler's Anniversary Discourse before the Albany Institute in* 1830, *p.* 54.

In the year 1776, again, no public commencement was held; but six students, who had just completed their course when the College was broken up, were admitted to the degree of Bachelor of Arts. The college record of this year remarks: "The turbulence and confusion which prevail in every part of the country effectually suppress every literary pursuit."

It would seem, however, that some instruction continued to be given under the auspices of King's

College, though not within its walls, for we find in its Matricula the names of William Walton and James Delancey Walton, entered in the year 1777; and the Governors appear to have met occasionally after this, for there exists a certified copy of minutes of a meeting on the 17th of May, 1781. These are the only indications, faint as they are, which have been discovered of the slumbering existence of the college during a period of eight years—from the spring of 1776 to that of 1784—except, that it afterwards appears from the minutes of the Trustees of Columbia College, on the 28th of March, 1788, that Mr. Moore, the President *ad interim*, occupied during a part of this period a house furnished by Mr. Lispenard for the use of the officers and students of the college, when the college edifice was converted into a hospital.

At the end of this period of eight years, during which the college remained in abeyance, as it were, the Legislature of New York, on the 1st of May, 1784, passed "An Act for granting certain privileges to the college heretofore called King's College, for altering the name and charter thereof, and erecting an University within this State."

The Regents of the University appointed by this Act held their first meeting only four days after the passing of it; but, for want of a quorum, adjourned to the day following, when they organized their Board by the appointment of Governor Clinton, as Chancellor; the Hon. Pierre Van Cortlandt, as Vice-Chancellor; Brockholst Livingston, as Treasurer; and Robert Harpur, as Secretary of the University. Mr. Livingston, who in the office to which he was now appointed continued to serve Columbia College zealously and faithfully during the long period of forty years, being a son of the gentleman who had so bitterly opposed King's College thirty years before; and Mr. Harpur, the same person who had seventeen years before resigned his professorship therein.

At this same meeting a committee was appointed "to demand and receive from the late corporation of the college called King's College" whatever property had belonged to it; and the Regents entered with laudable activity upon their task of setting in order the affairs of the revived institution, which by the recent Act was styled Columbia College. Among other measures for that purpose adopted at this first meeting, was the appointment of the Rev. John Peter Tetard as Professor of the French Language and the assignment of various important matters to several committees. One was charged with the repairs of the college edifice; another with the duty of engaging proper instructors; a third with that of devising a seal for the new corporation; a fourth with that of preparing by-laws for it; and a fifth with the care of sending a suitable person to solicit subscriptions in France and other parts of Europe. This last measure, and the appointment of a French Professor before any other, may be viewed as evidence of the more intimate relations subsisting between the now independent States and France.

On the 15th of the same month of May, the Regents resolved to institute a Grammar School in the college, and appointed Mr. William Cochran as master thereof, and also to be temporary teacher in the college, of the Greek and Latin Languages; of which, on the 23d of December following, he was elected Professor.

On the 17th of May, 1784, the first student of the college, under its new name and government, De Witt Clinton, presenting himself as a candidate for admission into the Junior Class, was examined, found qualified, and admitted accordingly by a committee of the Regents consisting of the Chancellor, Vice-Chancellor, and Secretary, the Mayor of New York, and the newly appointed professor Tetard. And in this manner, by a committee of the Regents, do all subsequent examinations appear to have been conducted, for so long as the college continued under their immediate care. During this period, which was of about three years, they seem to have been very zealous and active in their endeavors to place the college on a respectable footing—to make it, in fact, the nucleus of an institution which might deserve to be styled an University. With this view they applied themselves diligently to obtain subscriptions of money towards the maintenance of the college; and making large calculations, probably, on the success of these, they resolved, December 14th, 1784, to organize the four faculties of Arts, Divinity, Medicine, and Law, making the first to comprise seven professorships, the second to consist of such as might be established by the different religious societies within the State, pursuant to the Act instituting the University—the third to be composed of seven professors, and the last of three. Besides all which there were to be nine extra professors, a president, a secretary, and a librarian—and all this magnificent scheme was adopted when the entire income from the real and personal property of the college did not exceed the sum of twelve hundred pounds.

From the catalogue of the college it may be seen what professorships were, in fact, established at this time, or afterwards, while the college remained under the immediate superintendence of the Regents. During this period no president was appointed, but the duties of the office were discharged by the professors, in turn, and at the commencements held in 1786 and 1787, instead of diplomas, there were given under the seal of the corporation, and signed by the secretary, certificates that the parties receiving them were entitled to the degree of Bachelor of Arts.

This delay in appointing a President appears from a report adopted by the Regents, April 4th, 1785, to have been because the deranged state of the funds of the college, and the great losses it had sustained, rendered them unable to offer such a salary as would induce a suitable person to accept the office.

At length the Regents becoming sensible of the defective constitution of the University under the law from which they derived their authority; and a committee appointed to consider its state having, on the 15th of February, 1787, together with their report thereon, submitted the draft of a bill containing provisions calculated, as they thought, to remedy the defects of the actual system, the Regents adopted the report of this committee, and laid their bill, as amended by a subsequent committee, of which John Jay and Alexander Hamilton were members, before the Legislature of the State, which on the 13th of April following passed, accordingly, "An Act to institute an

University within this State, and for other purposes therein mentioned."

By the 8th, and some of the subsequent sections of this Act, which have reference to Columbia College, its original charter, with the necessary alterations, was confirmed, and it was placed under the care of twenty-nine gentlemen named in the Act as its Trustees, who were to exercise their functions until their number should be reduced by death, resignation, or removal from the State, to twenty-four, after which all vacancies in their number were to be filled by their own choice.

The first meeting of the Trustees of Columbia College was on the 8th of May, 1787, when they reappointed Robert Harpur and Brockholst Livingston to their respective offices of Clerk and Treasurer, and adopted, in so far as they were not repugnant to the present constitution of the college, the by-laws which had been established by the Regents for its government.

On the 21st of the same month of May, William Samuel Johnson, LL.D., son of the first president of King's College, was elected President, and on the 12th of November following, he signified to the Trustees his acceptance of the office.

At this time the Faculty of Arts and that of Medicine consisted, each, of three professors. There were no professors in the Faculties of Law and of Divinity, and the only extra professor was one of the German language, who received no salary. Of the thirty-nine students, (nearly one-half of them belonging to the Freshman Class,) five lodged and boarded in the college, and five others had rooms and studied there. The yearly income of the Institution was about one thousand three hundred and thirty pounds.

During the first four or five years after the re-organization of the college, there occurred scarcely any thing that deserves mention, except the resignation in 1789 of Mr. William Cochran, Professor of the Greek and Latin languages, and the appointment of Mr. Peter Wilson in his place.

One of the students in college, during these first years of its renewed existence, but who did not finish his course there, was John Randolph, of Mattoax, Virginia, at that time, but better known afterwards as of Roanoke. He and his brother, Theodoric, entered the Freshman Class in 1788, and were promoted to the Sophomore Class in 1789; after which Theodoric's name does not again occur; but John, as appears from the matricula, entered the Junior Class of the following year.

In February, 1792, the Trustees, acting on the suggestion of the Medical Society of the State, and in concert with the Regents of the University, established the Medical school of the college on a more respectable footing than before, by the appointment of a Dean of the Faculty of Medicine, and seven Medical Professors. Dr. Samuel Bard, who had been Professor of the Theory and Practice of Medicine in the first medical school established in the college in 1767, and more recently had held first the professorship of Chemistry, and then that of Natural Philosophy and Astronomy, while the college was governed by the Regents, was now elected Dean of the new Faculty, in which there were associated with him Doctors Baily, Post, Rodgers, Hamersley, Smith, Nicoll, and Kissam, all eminent in their profession.

Dr. Romaine, who had been giving lectures at the college on certain branches of medical science, having, on the organization of this new school, resigned his office, the rooms which had been used by him were arranged for its accommodation, such alterations being made therein as were required.

In April, 1792, the Rev. Elias D. Rattoon, on

the resignation of Professor Wilson, was chosen Professor of the Greek and Latin languages; and in May, 1794, received the further appointment of Professor of Grecian and Roman Antiquities. He resigned both offices on the 9th of June, 1797, and on the 19th of the same month, his predecessor, Dr. Wilson, was re-elected to fill them, as he thenceforth continued to do for three and twenty years.

Besides the establishment of a medical school, the Trustees gave further evidence, during the year 1792, of their desire to make the college useful and respectable, by filling several other professorships. Dr. Kunze was re-appointed Professor of Oriental Languages. Dr. Mitchill was chosen Professor of Natural History, Chemistry, Agriculture, and Botany: and M. de Marcelin, Professor of French. In the following year, 1793, Mr. James Kent was elected Professor of Law, and in 1795, the Rev. Dr. M'Knight was appointed Professor of Moral Philosophy and Logic, the Rev. John Bisset, A. M., of Aberdeen, Professor of Rhetoric and Belles-Lettres; and the professorship of Geography was assigned to Dr. Kemp, in addition to that of Mathematics and Natural Philosophy, which he already held.

Meanwhile the foundation of an additional building was, in conformity with the original plan of the college, laid at right angles to the then existing edifice, along the west side of the college green; and on the northern end of this foundation, in order to supply the more immediate wants of the institution, was begun a superstructure intended to contain a hall and several recitation rooms.

The Trustees were encouraged to the making of the appointments just now mentioned, the laying of this more extensive foundation than they were able to finish, and the purchase of a large addition to the college library, by a grant obtained from the Legislature in April, 1792, of £7,900, and of the further sum of £750 annually for five years. They soon discovered, however, that they had extended their views, and had proceeded in their plan of building farther than this addition to their means would warrant. In 1796 they were obliged again to ask for legislative aid to complete their edifice; and their application proving unsuccessful, the committee employed about the new building was empowered to proceed with it until the money granted for that purpose should be expended, and in June of the year following, was directed to sell the perishable building materials which then remained on hand.

The annual payment of £750 by the State being

discontinued on the expiration of the period of five years for which it had been granted, the additional professors, towards whose salaries that money had been applied, were found too burthensome, and consequently, in February, 1799, the duty of teaching Rhetoric and Belles-Lettres, Logic and Moral Philosophy, was devolved upon the President. Mathematics, Natural Philosophy and Geography were united under one professorship. The Latin and Greek Languages, Roman and Grecian Antiquities, were combined to form another. The professorships of the Oriental Languages, of French, and of Law, were discontinued. A professorship, however, of Natural History and Chemistry was instituted, and these studies were made to form part of the regular academic course.

On the 16th of July, 1800, Dr. Johnson, having nearly reached his 74th year, and feeling the infirmities of age, resigned his presidency and retired to Stratford. The tranquil life to which he was there restored, and the air of his native village, re-established in a great degree his bodily health, and in the enjoyment of a leisure so well earned by the professional toils and highly important public services of his previous long career, he lived to enter upon his 93d year, "retaining to the last his vigor and activity of mind, the ardor of his literary curiosity, and a most lively interest in whatever concerned the welfare of this country, and of the Christian world."

On Dr. Johnson's resignation the Trustees empowered the senior professor to preside at the ensuing commencement, and to confer the degrees that had been ordered.

On the 25th of May, 1801, the Rev. Dr. Wharton, of Philadelphia, was elected president, and, on the 3d of August, signified, by letter, his acceptance of the office, which, on the 11th of December following, he resigned.

It was now determined that the professorship which for about three years had been annexed to the presidential office, should be detached therefrom, and that the President, in future, should be charged merely with a general superintendence of the institution, the duty of attending at examinations, presiding at commencements, and performing such other acts as are more peculiar to his office. This change was adopted on the 30th of December, 1801, and on the following day the Right Rev. Benjamin Moore was appointed to the office of president, which he had held *ad interim* on the departure of Dr. Cooper, above six and twenty years before. At the same time the Rev. Dr. Bowden, who, like Bishop Moore, was an alumnus of the College, was appointed to the now distinct professorship of Moral Philosophy, Rhetoric and Belles-Lettres, and Logic.

Under this new arrangement the President was not expected to reside in the college, nor, on ordinary occasions, to take an active part in its discipline and government; the chief management of its daily concerns being committed to the professors. The plan was not a good one in itself; but Doctors Kemp, Wilson and Bowden, being highly respectable and able men, the college, notwithstanding, went on well, increasing in reputation and in number. Its funds derived some augmentation from a grant of lands made to it in 1802 by the Regents of the University; its real estate in the city was daily becoming more valuable; the hall and recitation rooms on the north end of the new foundation were completed; and though the remainder of that foundation (already falling to ruin) and the original college edifice presented a decayed and unsightly appearance, yet the internal condition of the institution, at this period, was not unprosperous.

And, except that its buildings were yearly growing worse, there was little change about the college, nor does its history offer anything that deserves especial notice until the 22d of June, 1809, when, upon the recommendation of a committee, consisting of Mr. Rufus King, and the

Reverend Doctors Mason, Abeel, Hobart, and Miller, a new regulation was adopted, whereby the requisites for admission into college, after the 1st of October, 1810, were raised much higher than they had ever been before; and in February following, the same committee, to which the Rev. Dr. Romeyn had in the interim been added, reported, also, a new course of studies and system of discipline within the college, in accordance with the new statute as to admission.

The adoption of the well-considered plans of this very able committee was calculated, and had the effect, greatly to elevate and extend our system of collegiate education.

In the spring of 1810 the Trustees obtained a new charter from the Legislature of the State, by which certain restrictions in the former charter were removed, and some defects therein, which experience had discovered, were supplied.

From the annual report to the Regents, in February, 1810, it appears that the number of students matriculated for that year was 135. The Trustees remark, that on comparing this with former reports, "the Regents will perceive that notwithstanding the many embarrassments with which she has to struggle, Columbia College not only maintains her ground, but increases her importance." They further observe, that they have prosecuted the theoretical and practical system of the college so far toward its results as "to lay a broader and stronger basis for sound and thorough education than (as they believe) has hitherto been known in these States."

The affairs of the institution being, in some respects, thus hopeful, and a great zeal for its advancement manifested, Bishop Moore, in May, 1811, resigned his presidency, in order to make room for some one who would have it in his power to devote himself wholly to the college; and, in the following month, the Trustees determined to divide the powers and duties of the presidential office between a president and an officer to be styled Provost, who, in the absence of the President, should supply his place, and who, besides exercising the like general superintendence with the President, should conduct the classical studies of the Senior Class. The statutes of the college were altered accordingly, and, on the 17th of June, 1811, the Rev. William Harris was elected President, and the Rev. Dr. Mason, Provost.

On the 14th of February, 1812, the Legislature, in accordance with the petition of the Trustees, passed an act making the Provost of the college for the time being eligible as a member of their Board, and, in May following, the Provost, Dr. Mason, was elected a Trustee.

On the 25th of November, 1812, Dr. Kemp died, after having, for eight and twenty years, discharged with great ability and fidelity the duties of professor of Mathematics and Natural Philosophy. The resolutions of the Trustees on this occasion manifest their high respect for his memory, and their concern for the loss which the college had sustained.

During the last illness of Dr. Kemp, and for some time after his decease, the duties of his office were divided between Mr. James Renwick, whose services were voluntarily and gratuitously rendered, and Mr. Henry Vethake, who had been engaged by the Trustees; but, on the 3d of May, 1813, Mr. Robert Adrain was elected to fill the vacant professorship. The purchase by the college of the late professor's books made a valuable addition to its library.

On the 1st of November, 1813, the Trustees agreed to incorporate their medical school with that of the College of Physicians and Surgeons, a new institution which the Regents of the University had established in the city of New York.

On the 11th of July, 1816, Dr. Mason resigned his office of Provost, and, on the 7th of November following, the Trustees determined that the powers and duties of that office should devolve upon the President, except that the duty of conducting the classical studies of the Senior Class should be restored to the Professor of the Greek and Latin Languages.

An attentive examination made into the state of their finances, having satisfied the Trustees that they might safely undertake extensive repairs of the old edifice, and the erection of additional buildings, they, on the 6th of September, 1817, agreed upon the general outlines of a plan for that purpose, and appointed a committee to carry it into effect.

Two wings, each fifty feet square, and each containing two houses for professors, were added at the extremities of the original edifice, and of this older building, which underwent very extensive alterations, one-fourth part being reserved as a dwelling-house, the residue was so arranged as to furnish a chapel, a library, and all the required recitation rooms.

Shortly before the adoption of this plan, the Rev. Dr. Bowden, who, for about sixteen years, had filled the office of Professor of Moral Philosophy, Rhetoric and Belles-Lettres, and Logic, died much lamented. The Trustees adopted resolutions which feelingly expressed their high sense of the long and faithful services of the deceased, and of the learning and ability with which he had discharged his professional duties, together with their veneration for the example displayed by him of all the moral and Christian virtues; and neither in this case nor in that of Dr. Kemp's death did they limit to words alone the evidence of their regard.

On the 3d of November, 1817, the Rev. John M'Vickar was appointed to the professorship which Dr. Bowden had held, and, at the same meeting, with a view to relieve Dr. Wilson of some portion of the duties which his advancing age began to render burthensome, it was resolved to appoint an adjunct professor of the Greek and Latin Languages. On the first day of the following month Mr. Nathaniel F. Moore was elected to that office, and charged with the duty of teaching those languages to the Freshman Class.

Meanwhile the improvements in the exterior of the college, and the additions that had been resolved upon, were going forward; but it was not until the 2d of October, 1820, that, the projected alterations being completed, the Building Committee handed in their final report. During the progress of the work, the Trustees received a valuable contribution towards it, by a grant from the State of $10,000; and the same Act, passed February 19th, 1819, added also to the value of the college property, by rescinding the condition of a grant which had been made five years before, of the Botanic Garden—a piece of some twenty acres of ground about three miles out of town—a condition requiring that the college should be removed to the land so granted within the next twelve years.

But the extensive additions and alterations about the college proved so expensive, that notwithstanding this legislative aid, a considerable debt had been incurred.

The Trustees, however, would not be deterred thereby from assuming new burthens, which either a just regard for the claims of one who had long served the college with fidelity, or the exigencies of its discipline and course of study, seemed to lay upon them. Accordingly, when Dr. Wilson found himself obliged by increasing infirmities wholly to resign his office, as in February, 1820, he did, they, in consideration of his "faithful and eminently useful services during eight and twenty years; of his advanced age, and the peculiar circumstances of his situation," granted him a liberal annuity for life. Being persuaded, moreover, that the welfare of the college required a division of the professorship of Mathematics and Natural Philosophy into a professorship of Mathematics and Astronomy, and a professorship of Natural and Experimental Philosophy and Chemistry, they resolved on such division accordingly; and, leaving Dr. Adrain charged with the former, appointed, on the 4th of December, 1820, Mr. James Renwick to the latter office. To that which Dr. Wilson had resigned, the adjunct professor, Mr. Nathaniel F. Moore, was, in February, 1820, preferred, and, on the 6th of the following month, Mr. Charles Anthon was appointed to supply his place.

The college, now for the first time, saw most of her offices filled by her own alumni—Professors M'Vickar, Moore, Anthon, and Renwick having all been reared within her walls, while previous to 1817, only three of all who had ever held office in the college had received their education there. These were the Rev. John Vardill—who probably never entered on the duties of his office—the Rev. Benj. Moore, and the Rev. John Bowden.

On the 3d of November, 1823, the Honourable James Kent was re-appointed to the professorship of Law, which he had five and twenty years before resigned, after having then held it five years. The present appointment of this accomplished jurist having given occasion to a course of lectures at the college, which proved the germ of his learned Commentaries, was, consequently, attended with results, which, while they reflect honour on the college, are of inestimable value to the science of jurisprudence, and the whole legal profession.

On the 5th of September, 1825, was established, for the first time in the college, a professorship of the Italian language and literature; to which the Trustees appointed Signor Lorenzo Da Ponte, a gentleman of singular talent, a scholar and poet of no ordinary merit.

On the 7th of November, in the same year, Dr. Adrain resigned his professorship of Mathematics and Astronomy. In the letter offering his resignation, he, in the warmest terms possible, recommended as his successor Henry J. Anderson, M. D., an alumnus of the college, who on the 11th of the same month was elected in his place.

In October, 1827, a new body of statutes for the government of the college was adopted, and in December of the same year the Trustees resolved to establish, under their patronage, a grammar school, of which the Board of the college should have the superintendence and control. The plan, however, failed altogether of success, until after it had received some modifications in the month of April following; nor, even then, did it, for a long time, succeed in any great degree. In the spring of 1829, measures were taken to erect a suitable building for its accommodation. This was finished and occupied in the month of October following, and the Trustees made an agreement with Mr.

John D. Ogilby, as master of the school, under the control and direction of the College Board.

In October, 1829, Dr. Harris died, after being in the presidential office for above eighteen years; but, with full charge of the college for only the last thirteen of them; during all which time he had manifested the most entire and zealous devotion to its interests.

On the 9th of December following his decease, the Honourable William A. Duer, LL. D., was elected in his place.

Early in 1830 extensive modifications of the college system were adopted—the existing course of study, being preserved entire, was denominated *the Full Course*, and another, in addition thereto, was established, which was called *the Scientific and Literary Course*—and this was open to others besides matriculated students; all persons whatever, and to such extent as they thought fit, being permitted to attend.

On the 3d of February, 1830, several new professors were appointed—viz: The Rev. Samuel H. Turner, D. D., was elected Professor of the Hebrew Language and Literature—Mariano Velesques de la Cadeña, Professor of the Spanish Language and Literature—the Rev. Manton Eastburn, Lecturer on Poetry, and Wm. H. Ellet, M.D., Lecturer on Elementary Chemistry.

In November, 1830, Professor Anthon took charge of the College Grammar School, as its Rector, under an agreement which was variously modified from time to time until the first of May, 1833, when the arrangement was concluded. Upon the appointment of Professor Anthon as Rector of the Grammar School, Mr. J. L. O'Sullivan was employed as classical instructor of the Freshman Class, and Dr. Ellet as instructor of the Sophomore Class in Elementary Chemistry; and in May, 1832, a distinct professorship of this department being established, Dr. Ellet was appointed to fill it. He held this appointment however, for only one year, when new arrangements, dictated by the necessity of reducing the expenses of the college, determined the Trustees to discontinue his professorship.

In October, 1835, Professor Moore having resigned his office, Dr. Anthon, the Jay-Professor (as since February, 1830, he had been styled) was elected in his place, and Mr. Robert G. Vermilye, an alumnus of the college, was appointed classical instructor of the Freshman Class, Librarian, and Secretary of the College Board.

On a revision of the statutes, in the year 1836, both courses of study pursued in the college were further enlarged; and the Scientific and Literary Course in particular was defined and materially extended. And in order that this course, as well as the scientific branches of the Full Course, might be conducted in the most efficient manner, the Trustees appropriated the sum of $10,000 for the purchase of additional apparatus, as well as for adding to the library the requisite books of reference and illustration.*

On the 13th of April, 1837, was celebrated, with much solemnity, the semi-centennial anniversary of the re-organization of the college under Trustees of its own. The Trustees, President, Professors, Alumni, and students of the college, united in measures calculated to give interest to the day. In the morning, at St. John's Chapel, an Oration and a Poem were delivered, before a numerous audience, by Alumni of the college previously appointed. Odes in several languages, composed and arranged to music for the occasion, were sung; there were suitable religious services, and appropriate music, and honorary degrees were conferred on several distinguished gentlemen, selected by a committee specially appointed for that purpose. In the evening the college was decorated, illuminated, and thrown open for the reception and

---

* During the preceding year, 1835, the Trustees had increased the means of instruction belonging to the college by the purchase of two collections of minerals, at an aggregate cost of $2,300, and subsequently there was added to their cabinet a valuable geological collection, presented by the State.

entertainment of a large number of invited guests.

In January, 1838, the Trustees made a valuable addition to the College Library by purchasing that of their former professor, Moore, whom they also appointed Librarian, and as such he was, for about a year, busily employed in making a new arrangement and a catalogue of the whole library, and placing this department of the college on a better and more serviceable footing than before. On his resignation, Mr. George C. Schaeffer was appointed in his place.

In May, 1842, President Duer found himself obliged, by severe and long-continued illness, to resign his office; and on the first of August following, Nathaniel F. Moore, LL. D., was appointed in his place.

In June, 1843, Dr. Anderson resigned the professorship of Mathematics and Astronomy, and in the following month the Rev. Charles W. Hackley, S. T. D., was appointed in his place.

In April, 1843, a professorship of the German Language and Literature was established on an endowment of $20,000, bequeathed for that purpose by Frederick Gebhard, Esq., and in the month of June following, John Louis Tellkampf, J. U. D., of Gottingen, was appointed *Gebhard Professor*.

On a revision of the statutes in July, of this year,

the *Scientific and Literary Course*, after an unsuccessful experiment of thirteen years, was finally abolished. As distinguished from the *Full Course*, it had never found much favor with the public. There was not a single student engaged in it at this time, and during the last two years there had been, in all, but four.

At the same time that the revision of the statutes was made, the Trustees directed that the German Language and Literature should be made a part of the College course; and at the beginning of the second session of the following year, Professor Tellkampf began the instruction of his classes. Difficulties, however, which had not been wholly unanticipated, interfered with the success of the new arrangement. In October, 1847, Professor Tellkampf resigned his position and was succeeded, on the first of November of the same year by the Reverend Henry I. Schmidt, who still holds the office. In January, 1847, the attendance of the two higher classes was made voluntary, and that arrangement continued in force till 1857, when the study of German was made wholly voluntary; and to guard against the possibility of the department's sinking into a sinecure, four annual prizes, two of $30 each and the others of $20, were instituted. This arrangement is still in force, and has been found to work well. About one-fourth of the students avail themselves of the instruction of the Gebhard Professor, and pursue their studies with energy and vigor, and the liberal intentions of the founder of the Professorship are fairly carried out.

Upon the resignation of Professor Vermilye, in 1843, the instruction of the Senior Class in Greek and Latin was intrusted to the President, and the Freshmen were required to attend Professor Anthon. This arrangement subsisted, however, but for a single session; and in the month of April following, Dr. Anthon resumed the instruction of the Senior Class; while Mr. Henry Drisler, an alumnus of the College, who had, since the resignation of Mr. Vermilye, aided in the instruction of the Freshman Class, took entire charge of the classical studies of that class, first as Tutor and afterwards as Adjunct Professor.

In October, 1847, Mr. Schaeffer resigned his office as Librarian, having accepted a professorship in Danville College, Kentucky, and his assistant, Mr. Lefroy Ravenhill, was appointed in his place; and two years later, Mr. Stephen R. Weeks, the Janitor of the College, was made Assistant Librarian, upon the recommendation of President Moore.

In December, 1844, Mr. J. W. S. Hows was appointed Professor of Elocution, with the duty of giving instruction therein to the Freshman Class, and in January, 1845, entered upon his duties. In 1848, William Betts, A. M., an alumnus and Trustee of the College, was elected Professor of Law, in the room of Chancellor Kent, who had died not long before. In the winter of 1849–50, Mr. Betts delivered, in the College, a course of Lectures on International Law. In July, 1849, Dr. Moore resigned the presidency, and in the following month of November, Charles King, Esquire, was elected his successor.

The rapid growth of the city and the falling in of the lease of the Botanic Garden directed the attention of the Trustees early in 1850 to the consideration of the disposition of that portion of their property. The Botanic Garden was a tract containing about 260 lots of ground, bounded on the north by 51st St., on the south by 47th St., on the east by the 5th Avenue, and on the west by a line nearly parallel to and about a hundred feet distant from the 6th Avenue. It had been given to the college by the State of New York, in 1814, as a partial compensation for the large estate in Gloucester County, which she had lost when Vermont was made a State. It had for many years brought in a trifling revenue, which had long been wholly inadequate to meet even the expenses in which it had involved the college; and now it seemed about to make still more formidable demands upon her resources to meet taxes, assessments, and the cost of regulating the lots. The whole subject of the disposition of this property was one of extreme delicacy and difficulty, and occupied the careful attention of the Trustees for nearly two years. It was finally leased, and so judiciously that it has now become one of the best parts of the city.

Dr. Ravenhill dying in 1851, William Alfred Jones, A. M., was appointed his successor, and held the office of Librarian for more than 14 years. On the 14th of November, 1854, Dr. Renwick resigned his professorship. At the same time, an order of Emeritus Professors was instituted, for the purpose of appropriately acknowledging the services of those professors who had devoted themselves to the college for twenty years or more, and Dr. Renwick was made the first Emeritus Professor. These gentlemen were to be without salaries or stated duties, but were to have certain privileges and honors, the principal of which were these: Each of them was to have the right of nomination to one free scholarship to be called by his name, of delivering an annual lecture in the college, and of sitting with the Faculty on public occasions. His portrait also was to be painted at the expense of the college, and hung in the library or in some proper room in the college buildings. Since Dr. Renwick, three other gentlemen have received this honor, viz.: the Rev. Dr. John McVickar, made Emeritus Professor of the Evidences of Natural and Revealed Religion, in 1864, after an active service of 47 years; Dr. Charles Davies, in 1865, Emeritus Professor of Higher Mathematics; and Dr. Henry James Anderson, in 1866, Emeritus Professor of Mathematics and Astronomy,—the rule requiring twenty years' service having been suspended in the case of Drs. Anderson and Davies.

On the 4th of April, 1854, Richard S. McCulloh, A. M., then a Professor in Princeton College, N. J., was elected Professor of Natural and Experimental Philosophy and Chemistry.

The requirements of commerce rendered necessary the removal of the college from College Place; and in 1857 it was removed to the block which it now occupies, bounded by 49th and 50th Sts., 4th and Madison Avenues. The old college buildings have long ceased to exist, and the College Green is transformed into streets lined with costly warehouses.

The working out of the plan of enlarging the scope of instruction given by the college went on simultaneously with that for the removal of its site. Both subjects, indeed, had been in the hands of a committee since 1853, for it was found that the two could not be separated. Thus, although the committee presented their final report as early as 1854, their suggestions could not be immediately carried into practice. Unexpected and inevitable delays arose in finding accommodations in the upper part of the town, and the old college had just sufficient room for the body of professors that taught and the course of instruction that was carried on within its walls. When, however, the removal of the college was completed, it became possible to carry out in part the plan which had been suggested by the committee and adopted by the Trustees. That plan contemplated the preservation of the "Classical course as at present established for three years; that is, the Freshman, Sophomore and Junior, with adaptations, however, to the future studies, both sub-graduate and post-graduate; and a co-ordinate, mainly scientific course, with due regard to classical and ethical instruction, to occupy two years, and a third when the demand shall justify it. These two courses, proceeding in nearly parallel lines, were to meet at the commencement of the Senior year, and the students to be prepared to undertake any of the studies to be thereafter taught." (Report of the Committee on the Course, July 24, 1854.) Three schools--viz.: of Philosophy or Philology, of Jurisprudence and History, and a school of Mathematical and Physical Science—were to be instituted, into one of which the students were to enter at the beginning of the fourth or Senior year, and at the end of that year those who had pursued the earlier classical course were to receive the degree of Bachelor of Arts, and those who had pursued the scientific course that of Bachelor of Science. The studies of these schools, however, were not to end with the first degree, but were to continue for two years longer, and to form what was to be called the post-graduate course. This scheme, admirable as it was in conception, was never fully carried out. Several professors were, indeed, added to the Faculty in 1857, and the Senior Class was divided into schools, called the Schools of Letters, Jurisprudence and Science, as had been proposed by the committee; but the post-graduate course, as contemplated by the committee, never had any existence. The committee in charge of the subject were authorized, by resolutions of the Board of Trustees, June 28, 1858, to open the post-graduate course of instruction on the first Monday of November following, to secure the services, "for such portions of the next two years as they may be able," of Professor James D. Dana, in the department of Geology and Natural History; of Professor Arnold Guyot, in

Physical Geography and kindred subjects; of Mr. George P. Marsh, in the English Language; of Professor Theodore W. Dwight, for the Law Department, and of such other instructors as the committee might deem proper, under the instructions given them, in any department of Jurisprudence, Science or Letters. Professors of the college were also to give their aid. In the Fall of 1858, the course was opened and continued for one year. Professor Guyot delivered a course of lectures on Comparative Physical Geography in its relation to History and Modern Civilization; Mr. Marsh a course upon the English Language; Professor William G. Peck upon Engineering in all its branches; Professor Charles W. Hackley upon Physical Astronomy; and Professor Charles Murray Nairne upon Ethics and Moral Philosophy. But the time seemed not to be ripe for the proper support by the public of the scheme, and it was relinquished after one year's trial. The college indeed by no means abandoned its cherished plan of giving more than ordinary academic training; but professional and scientific schools superseded that more liberal and extended course of teaching, by which it had been hoped to inspire young men with an ardent and honorable love of learning, and to qualify them for those "higher and more arduous efforts of self-instruction" which the college has ever regarded as the true aim and purpose of academic training.

The chairs held by Professors McVickar, McCulloh and Hackley were divided in 1857, with the consent and approbation of the gentlemen who held them. The duties of the former two, indeed, had become too onerous to be discharged by a single man, however earnest and energetic he might be. The professorships held by Professor McVickar were divided into three, viz: a chair of the Evidences of Natural and Revealed Religion, which the professor himself retained; a chair of Moral and Intellectual Philosophy and Literature, which was filled by the election of Charles Murray Nairne, A. M.; a chair of History and Political Science, to which Francis Lieber, LL. D., was elected. About the same time, Charles A. Joy, Ph. D., was made Professor of Chemistry, it being the purpose of Professor McCulloh, with the approbation and by the direction of the Trustees, to confine himself to the department of Physical Science. Professor Hackley took the chair of Astronomy, and Charles Davies, LL. D., was made Professor of Mathematics.

The Professorship of Law, which had formerly been held by Chancellor Kent, and to which Mr. Betts was elected in 1848, had long existed in name only. Neither of these gentlemen had, indeed, attempted anything more than to deliver a single course of lectures; and after the chair had been vacated by the withdrawal of Mr. Betts, in 1854, it was not again filled. In 1858, however, it was determined to make the Department of Law an efficient and active portion of the college, and to combine it with the School of Jurisprudence in such a manner as that, while it should be a real preparation for practice at the bar, it should also give instruction in such kindred subjects as History, the Science of Government and International and Constitutional Law. Accordingly, on the 17th of May, 1858, Theodore W. Dwight, A. M., was made Instructor in Municipal Law, and afterwards promoted to be Professor and placed at the head of the Department, with the title of Warden of the Law School. Instruction in Constitutional Law was given by Professor Lieber, and in Moral Philosophy by Professor Nairne. John Ordronaux, M. D., was made Professor of Medical Jurisprudence. Courses of Lectures were delivered by several distinguished legal gentlemen of New York, who liberally gave their services without remuneration. The result of these energetic measures was that at the first commencement in May, 1860, twenty-eight students received the degree of LL. B., and the next year there were sixty-three students in the Law School. The number of students has steadily increased, and in the present year (1875–6) there are 573 in attendance.

In 1860, an arrangement was made by which the College of Physicians and Surgeons of the City of New York—an institution chartered by the Regents of the University of the State of New York, in 1807, and with which the Medical School of Columbia College was incorporated in 1813—was adopted as the Medical Department of the College.

Dr. Hackley dying in 1861, the Department of Astronomy was entrusted to Mr. William G. Peck, a graduate of the U. S. Military Academy, who had been, 1857–9, adjunct Professor of Mathematics, and since 1859 Professor of Pure Mathematics. On the third of June, in the same year, the division of the Senior Class into schools was abolished, and it was directed that all the students of that class should thenceforth follow the same course of study. In 1864, the Senior Class was allowed an option between the classics and higher mathematics; and in 1872, this option was extended so that since that time choice may be made between Greek and higher mathematics; Latin and higher Physics; Psychology and higher Chemistry—the required studies for the whole class being Organic Chemistry and Geology; Astronomy; Optics and Acoustics; Economics; Philosophical Essays.

Early in the year 1863, Mr. Thomas Egleston, Jr., prepared a plan for the establishment of a School of Mines and Metallurgy in connection with the college. In the course of the year 1864, the plan proposed by Mr. Egleston was adopted by the Trustees, and arrangements were made for establishing a School of Mines under his direction. Mr. Egleston was made Professor of Mineralogy and Metallurgy, and shortly afterwards Brig. Gen. Francis L. Vinton was made Professor of Mining Engineering. With this force, augmented by the addition of Charles F. Chandler, Ph. D., as Professor of Analytical and Applied Chemistry, the School of Mines was formally opened on the 15th of November, 1864, in rooms assigned to it in the college buildings. Arrangements were made by which Professors Joy, Peck, Van Amringe, and Rood, of the College Faculty, were to give instruction in the School. In 1866, a Chair of Geology and Palæontology was created and filled by the appointment of Dr. John S. Newberry, a gentleman who had acquired much experience and reputation in the subjects assigned him. The number of students in the School increased so rapidly that it was soon found necessary to provide additional accommodations for them; and, accordingly in the year following the establishment of the School, a building was fitted up for its especial use. This building was found the next year to be inadequate, and a new and larger one was erected. In 1874, the older portions of the buildings occupied by the school were replaced by a large and costly structure, planned with special reference to the purposes of the school. The nucleus of a mineralogical collection was formed by a valuable donation of minerals made by George T. Strong, Esq., and this was soon afterwards enlarged by the gift from the Hon. Gouverneur Kemble, of a larger similar collection. Dr. Newberry also brought with him his magnificent geological and palæontological collection, which is one of the most perfect in existence, and in fossil botany surpasses every other known. The collections of the School have been greatly enlarged by purchases, gifts and exchanges, and are now among the most complete in the United States.

In this connection it seems proper to mention the Herbarium presented to the college by the late Professor John Torrey. This elegant collection, of which more particular mention will be made hereafter, is peculiarly rich in *type specimens*, and is much resorted to by botanists of the vicinity and from a distance. Professor Torrey presented, also, to the college his extensive and valuable Botanical Library.

On the 21st of December, 1863, Ogden M. Rood, A. M., was elected Professor of Mechanics and Physics in the place of Mr. McCulloh, who was expelled from his professorship, October 15, 1863, "for having abandoned his post and joined the Rebels." Early in the next year President King sent in his resignation, and on the 18th of May ensuing, the Rev. Frederick A. P. Barnard, S. T. D., LL. D., some time Chancellor of the University of Mississippi, was elected his successor. Dr. Barnard entered upon his duties in June, 1864, and on the 3d of the following October delivered his inaugural address in the college chapel. Mr. Jones, the Librarian, retiring in 1865, the Rev. Beverley R. Betts, A. M., succeeded him. Under the administration of Mr. Jones, and for several years before his time, much attention was paid to the Library. The Library had, indeed, never been neglected; but while the income of the college was small, the sums that could be appropriated to it were necessarily limited. With increased appropriations, however, it has been found possible not only to keep its older accumulations in almost perfect order, but also to add to it by degrees many works of great and permanent value. The College Library was never large, but it is choice and select. Since the establishment of the Schools of Law and Mines, many books have been removed to those schools. This, however, is regarded as a temporary arrangement, rendered necessary by the fact that the Law School is at a distance from the college, and that the members of the School of Mines desire the use of certain books at hours at which they could not conveniently have access to the College Library. A handsome collection of German books was added in 1843 to the College Library by the liberality of Professor Tellkampf, who selected them with great care in Germany.

Dr. Anthon died in 1867, after a service of forty-seven years; and Professor Drisler—who, like his instructor and friend, Dr. Anthon, had given the labor of his life to the college—was transferred from the chair of Latin to that of Greek. Charles Short, LL. D., some time President of Kenyon College, in Ohio, succeeded him as Professor of Latin. In May, 1868, two prizes of $300 and $150 respectively, for proficiency in Greek, were established by the Trustees. These were to be contended for at the end of the Junior year, and the examinations were to be upon an entire play of Æschylus, Sophocles, or Euripides, which had not been read in the college course.

In 1864, Professor McVickar retired from active employment and was made Emeritus Professor. His department was committed to the President.

In 1865, Professor Davies was made Emeritus Professor, and his department was committed to Professor Peck, assisted by Mr. J. Howard Van Amringe, A. M., an alumnus of the college, who was appointed Tutor in 1860, was made Adjunct Professor in 1863, and in June, 1873, was made Professor of Mathematics. At the same time (1865) Professor Lieber was transferred to the Law School, and his duties in the college were entrusted to Professor Nairne, with a Tutor. Dr. Lieber died in 1872, and the chair of "Constitutional History and Public Law" has not since been filled.

In 1871, two fellowships in Literature and Science, open upon certain conditions to members of the graduating class, each of the annual value of $500, to be held for three years, were instituted; and at the same time, six scholarships in Classics and Mathematics were established in the Freshman and Sophomore classes, and the like number in the Junior class, in Latin, in Logic and English Literature, in History and Rhetoric, in Chemistry, in Mechanics and in Physics. The next year this scheme was remodeled by dividing the scholarships in the Sophomore and Freshman classes by adding in the latter class a scholarship in Rhetoric, and in the Junior class one in Greek, and by so rearranging the whole as to make fourteen instead of twelve scholarships, each of the annual value of one hundred dollars.

Columbia College has, at the present time, a Faculty of Arts, a Faculty of Law, a Faculty of Medicine, and a Faculty of Mining and General Science, embracing a President and eighty-seven Professors and other instructors, and, in all the Departments, thirteen hundred and sixty-one students.

School of Law—Columbia College.

The Law School of Columbia College, in its present form, was established in New York city in the year 1858. There had been, at an early day, courses of law lectures delivered by a distinguished jurist and professor in the college, Chancellor Kent. These had attracted much attention, and had been of great service in fitting students to practice at the bar. They had been for many years wholly discontinued, and at the time referred to (1858) there was no systematic instruction in law given by any public institution in the city. The fundamental purpose sought to be attained by the existing organization was to give to students of law a more systematic and comprehensive course of instruction than was to be obtained by the ordinary methods of legal education which then prevailed. Though a few law schools were then in existence in other parts of the country, they attracted no considerable body of students, and legal training and admission to the bar were commonly sought through the avenue of the lawyer's office. The inadequacy of this mode of preparation to furnish a proper professional education, affording, as it did, no regular, thorough and well-graded course of legal studies, was believed to render necessary and expedient the establishment of a system of institutional instruction similar to that adopted in academic colleges in teaching other branches of learning. One of the chief objects in view was to impart to the study of jurisprudence a more distinctively scientific character, and to inculcate a knowledge of legal principles by the constant drill of oral recitation on the part of the students, and by familiar expositions given by thoroughly qualified instructors. In the adoption of this method of instruction by daily recitation, the custom, usually observed at that time and subsequently in similar institutions, of teaching by the mere reading of lectures to the students, was designedly much qualified, and this essential feature of the plan upon which the school was founded has, until within a comparatively recent time, constituted its distinguishing characteristic, as compared with other law schools. The anticipated advantages to be derived from the system adopted have been abundantly justified in actual experience. The school was organized under the immediate supervision and control of Professor Theodore W. Dwight, who was appointed Warden of the School and Professor of Municipal Law, and who has remained at its head until the present time. Previously to 1858, he had been connected for several years as Professor of Law with Hamilton College, in Clinton, N. Y., from which he was called to assume this position. A regular curriculum of studies in the various subjects of municipal law was arranged by him which should give to the students a thorough knowledge of the principles of all important topics of law and of general jurisprudence. With him were associated to form the Faculty of the Law School, Professors Francis Lieber and Charles M. Nairne, who were also members of the Faculty of the academic department of the college, and in 1860 there was added to this number Dr. John Ordronaux, as Professor of Medical Jurisprudence. The school was located at a distance from the college, so as to be nearer the business portion of the city, and more convenient of access to students, many of whom are connected with lawyers' offices while pursuing their studies in the school, and have, therefore, to come from the lower portion of the city. During the first year the exercises were held at the rooms of the Historical Society, on Eleventh street, but at the commencement of the ensuing year the school was located in Lafayette Place, directly opposite the Astor Library, which continued to be its location until the Fall of 1873, when, more ample accommodations becoming necessary, the present location (8 Great Jones street) was chosen. Professor Leiber's connection with the school continued until his death, in the summer of 1872, and he gave yearly a course of lectures upon those special subjects in which he had gained great distinction for his learning, originality and independence of thought, extensive research and sound judgment, viz.: the History of Political Literature, Political Ethics, the origin, development, objects and history of Political Society, Constitutional Government, etc. Since his death, his place has been temporarily filled by special lecturers, delivering courses of lectures upon the cognate subjects of political science, civil polity and international law, among whom have been included Hon. George H. Gusman, formerly U. S. Consul to Denmark, Charles W. McLean and Professor John W. Burgess, of Amherst College. It is expected, however, that a professor will soon be elected to occupy, permanently, this vacant chair. Professor Nairne is still assigned to the position of lecturer upon the Ethics of Jurisprudence. Professor Ordronaux delivers an annual course of lectures on Medical Jurisprudence, including personal and domestic relations, physically considered, and the subject of insanity, in all its bearings, civil as well as criminal, upon legal responsibility. In April, 1875, the number of the Faculty was further increased by the election of George Chase, Esq., as Assistant Professor of Municipal Law. The first class connected with the school numbered thirty-five (35), and the number has been constantly increasing, until at the present time (1876) the entire membership of the school is five hundred and seventy-three (573), of whom two hundred and fifty-one (251) belong to the Senior class, and three hundred and twenty-two (322) to the Junior class. The statistical table, published near the end of this article, exhibits the uniform progress and growth of the school.

With this brief historical sketch, it is now proper to refer to the present condition of the institution. The regular and systematic instruction of the students upon the various topics of legal science is under the control of Professor Dwight. The plan of instruction combines the study of selected textbooks, with lectures. The student is expected to prepare himself each day upon a topic assigned by the professor. He is then examined upon the subject studied. Having grappled with some of its difficulties, he is prepared for the full oral exposition which accompanies an examination. He is encouraged at the same time to ask questions upon any difficulties which may have suggested themselves to him. Written lectures are also given, in which the principles of law are succinctly stated and leading authorities are cited for further information. Under this system, the attention of the student is actively aroused, and he is prepared to pursue with eagerness such avenues of legal knowledge as may be open to him. It is believed that most of the young men who commence the study of law in this country need the training and discipline which a thorough and systematic course of drill and daily examination may furnish them. The instruction in the other departments consists mainly of lectures, with references to approved text-books and authorities. Courses of lectures are also delivered by Professor Dwight, as supplementary to the regular course of instruction, upon the various topics of Municipal Law. Series of lectures are given annually upon Political Science, International Law, the History, Development and Character of Constitutional Government, Medical Jurisprudence, &c., as has been previously stated. Professor Chase delivers yearly courses of lectures upon Criminal Law, the Law of Torts, and upon Pleading.

The course of study occupies two years, and is so arranged that a complete view is given during each year of the subjects embraced within it. The plan of instruction includes the various branches of common law, equity, commercial, international, and constitutional law, and especial attention is given to all topics embraced within the rule of the Supreme Court of New York, prescribing the studies requisite for admission to the bar. The first year is occupied with the study of general commentaries upon municipal law, of the law of contracts, and of real estate. The second year includes equity, jurisprudence, commercial law, the law of torts, criminal law, evidence, pleading and practice. It is expected that a third year, or post-graduate course, will soon be organized for those students who may desire to pursue their studies beyond the regular course. Each of the two classes is divided into two divisions, each of which occupies ten hours with the Professor of Municipal Law in each week. Any student may join either division of his class as he may prefer. The hours of attendance in the department of Municipal Law are at 9:30 A. M., 11 A. M., 3 and 4:30 P. M. The other lectures do not generally exceed three in each week. There are no exercises in the school on Saturdays.

The library of the school is open for the use of the students during the term, from 9 o'clock A. M. to 10 o'clock P. M., when those who desire it pursue their studies, especially in the preparation of cases for the moot court. The central position of the school renders it easily accessible. It is quite near the Astor Library, to which students have access, and the law department of which contains several thousand volumes, including a very extensive series of English and American reports, with a valuable and rare collection of works on foreign law, and a full collection of French cases, ancient and modern.

By a statute of the college, going into effect in 1876, a preliminary examination has been required as a qualification for admission under the following provisions: graduates of literary colleges are admitted without examination; other candidates for admission must be at least eighteen years of age, and have received a good academic education, including such a knowledge of the Latin language as is required for admission to the Freshman Class of this college--viz.: four books of Cæsar's "Commentaries *de bello Gallico*," six books of Virgil's "Æneid," and six orations of Cicero. All applicants must be of good moral character.

The tuition fees are $100 per year, payable in

advance, which will admit the students to all the lectures and to the use of the Law Library.

Two moot courts are held every week, at each of which a cause previously assigned is argued by six or eight students. One week after the argument, an opinion upon the cause is delivered by the Professor presiding. The students are encouraged to take active part in these discussions, as an invaluable means of acquiring a knowledge of the law reports, and of becoming practically familiar with the preparation of briefs, the collection of authorities, and the decision of important litigated questions.

There has also been established in the school a series of prizes in the department of Municipal Law, to be awarded to those members of the graduating class in each year who have exhibited the greatest proficiency and excellence. These prizes are three in number: the first of $250, the second of $150, and the third of $100. The competitors for these prizes must have pursued the full course of study prescribed by the rules of the School. The examination is conducted by means of written essays upon a selected subject, and by written answers to a large variety of printed questions upon various topics of law; the adjudication of the prizes is made by a committee of three prominent members of the legal profession practising at the New York bar. The award is determined by the combined excellence of the essays and of the written answers to the examination questions. In deciding upon the comparative merit of the contestants, the clearness, vigor, and comprehensiveness of reasoning exhibited, the accuracy of statement, extent of learning, and conciseness and elegance of expression shown, are made the chief distinguishing tests. These prize examinations have been of the greatest value in promoting soundness and precision of scholarship, closeness of application, independent study and research, and have encouraged a salutary emulation in laying broad and deep the foundations of legal knowledge. A single prize of $150 per annum has been also recently established in the department of Political Science by Robert N. Toppan, Esq., of New York.

The admission of students to the bar is regulated as follows: An examination for degrees is held at the close of the Senior year before the professors of the Law School and the Law Committee of the Trustees, occupying four days and extending over all the studies of the course. The degree of Bachelor of Laws is conferred upon such students as shall have pursued, to the satisfaction of the Trustees and the Professors of Municipal Law, the entire course of study, and shall have passed the requisite examination. By the laws of the State, graduates of the Law School, having been in attendance for eighteen months, are admitted to practice in all the courts of the State on receiving the college diploma. They are admitted directly, without further examination as to their legal attainments, on proper application to the court, on furnishing satisfactory evidence of their good moral character. A student of the school who remains a year or more, but not sufficiently long to graduate, is entitled to an allowance of one year in making up the time required of clerks in offices by rule of court, as preliminary to his admission. This time is three years. An official certificate of the time of his attendance is given him on proper application to the Warden of the Law School.

The following table exhibits the number of students connected with the school since its organization:

	Seniors.	Juniors.	Total.
1858–59	35	..	35
1859–60	28	35	63
1860–61	61	42	103
1861–62	79	38	117
1862–63	90	56	146
1863–64	99	72	171
1864–65	93	77	170
1865–66	61	119	180
1866–67	92	78	170
1867–68	78	102	180
1868–69	97	107	204

	Seniors.	Juniors.	Total.
1869–70	95	135	230
1870–71	119	124	243
1871–72	124	167	291
1872–73	162	209	371
1873–74	198	240	438
1874–75	231	291	522
1875–76	251	322	573

The advantages of an education in a law school, as compared with other modes of obtaining a knowledge of legal principles and of securing admission to the bar, have, it is believed, been abundantly and unquestionably demonstrated by the experience of this school, and by the great success which it has achieved in point of numbers and influence. Its students are gathered from all parts of the United States, and there have been not a few in attendance, during the successive years of its existence, who have come from foreign countries. An institution of this kind, therefore, exerts a very wide and beneficial influence in elevating the standard of legal scholarship, in bringing into deserved prominence the scientific aspects of the study of jurisprudence, and in successfully inculcating a high grade of professional ethics. The particular benefits of a course of study in such an institution may be more specifically stated in the following terms:

(1.) They give the student a general and systematic outline of legal principles.

(2.) They remove out of the way difficulties inherent in the subject, from its vast extent, and its technical and scientific phraseology.

(3.) As a consequence, they tend to produce clearness of conception on the student's part, and lead him to carefulness and precision in expression.

(4.) They furnish for him during his professional career a supply of legal rules, which are so fixed in his memory that they can be continuously and confidently referred to for illustration, and as a basis for deductions, thus making it unnecessary to burden the memory with specific cases.

(5.) They inspire hope, courage, and enthusiasm in the student's progressive acquaintance with a science which is not only vast, but, as ordinarily acquired, dreary, and which can still be made interesting and attractive if it is pursued in the natural manner of first grasping principles and then considering details. It is of the greatest consequence that there is always at hand a trained lawyer in the person of his professor, to whom the student can go when in doubt, and ask such questions and seek such explanations as will cause his doubts to be removed.

(6.) Law Schools make the student acquainted with reports of law cases, ancient as well as modern, and their comparative value; teach him how to study the cases reported, and to apply legal rules to them, and thus give him an invaluable key to the great mass and volume of legal knowledge, which, from many who do not attend them, is wholly hidden. Next to perfect familiarity with a legal rule is the knowledge where to find it speedily when wanted, and this acquisition of a lifetime is most satisfactorily begun in the precincts of a law school.

(7.) They inspire a desire for communication and discussion with one's fellows. Under the guidance of the professors, the students tend to form societies for improvement by debate and mutual questioning. Moot courts are founded, kindly feeling is promoted, as well as professional courtesies and amenities. Solid friendships are formed, out of which springs a healthy regard for the good opinion of one's associates. Trickery and artifice, and sharp practice generally, are discouraged; a sound moral tone prevails, and professional ethics are promoted.

(8.) Most of all, law schools tend to prevent students from becoming mere technical lawyers—sticklers for form and critics of syllables; and to inspire them with a love for broad principles, and a corresponding aversion to all modes, however current, of spending time and talents in begetting and abetting knavery. To an ingenuous mind, nothing can be more delightful than the act of tracing the principles of jurisprudence historically, from their germs in the early conditions of our race down to the present time. It is these fundamental and underlying principles of law which the law schools seek after, digging for them as for hidden treasure. Learning, history, philosophy and ethics must be brought to bear upon students, and they must be taught diligently to "inquire of the sages not only to know the law, but the reason thereof."

(9.) It should be added that law schools adopt substantially the same methods of instruction as prevail in American literary colleges, and make use of the familiar oral exposition, or the more formal lecture, or rapid and persistent questioning, or apt illustration, and, in fact, use all the forms of the higher education to quicken and vivify the mind, and to cause instruction to be interesting and its results permanent. All the better educated young men naturally seek them. Their general culture leads them to delight in principle. The law school thus becomes a prolongation of the college, and its influence extends far forward into the student's professional career.

School of Mines—Columbia College.

Prior to the year 1864 there was no school in the United States in which mining was taught as a science. There were, in several institutions, nominal chairs of Mining Engineering; but it is nevertheless true that, up to the date noted, the young men of the country went abroad for their technical education in this department. The Columbia College School of Mines was founded in 1864, and was established for the distinctive purpose of furnishing to persons who desired it the means of acquiring a thorough scientific and practical knowledge of those branches of science which relate to mining, and of supplying to those engaged in mining and metallurgical operations persons competent to take charge of new or old works, and conduct them on thoroughly scientific principles.

In March, 1863, Mr. Thomas Egleston, a graduate of the *Ecole des Mines* of Paris, prepared a "Plan for a School of Mines and Metallurgy in New York City," and so far interested the trustees of Columbia College in it that they consented to make it, under certain conditions, a branch of the college—the essential condition being that the school was not to be a burden upon the funds of the college, but was to rely for its maintenance upon the liberal contributions which Mr. Egleston had been encouraged to expect from friends of science in the City of New York.

In January, 1864, Mr. Egleston was appointed Professor of Mineralogy and Metallurgy, and two rooms in the college building were assigned him, with an appropriation of five hundred dollars to fit them up.

The Rev. Dr. F. A. P. Barnard, who became President of the college shortly after Mr. Egleston's appointment, saw at once signs of promise in the newly inaugurated school; and it was chiefly his enlightened spirit, foresight, judgment and devotion that established it upon a firm basis, carried it through the most critical period of its existence, and finally expanded and developed it, until, in the thoroughness and scope of its teaching, it is believed to be unsurpassed by any professional school in this country or abroad.

Early in 1864, General Francis L. Vinton—who, like Professor Egleston, was a graduate of the *Ecole des Mines* of Paris—was appointed Professor of Mining Engineering; and a few months later Professor C. F. Chandler, of Union College, was made Professor of Analytical and Applied Chemistry.

The question of ways and means soon became a very embarrassing one. The expected endowment from friends of science was not obtained, and the school suffered for want of apparatus, chemicals, and the other appliances necessary for practical instruction in science. The committee of trustees in charge of the School and their associates were, by the terms of their appointment, not at liberty to apply to the trustees, and if they had been, the finances of the college itself were in a somewhat straitened condition. In this emergency, several gentlemen — among whom Mr. George T. Strong, Dr. John Torrey, and Mr. William E. Dodge, Jr., were most prominent— contributed three thousand dollars to equip a small laboratory, and thus to permit the opening of the school. The professors themselves were of course unpaid, except so far as they might derive compensation from the fees of students. Professors Joy, Peck, Van Amringe, and Rood, of the Academic Department, lent their aid to make the course of instruction complete. Rooms were assigned for the laboratory in the basement of the main college, where one was arranged capable of accommodating twelve students, and on the 15th of November, 1864, the school was opened. Twenty-five students entered on the opening day (twice as many as could be accommodated), and the numbers reached forty-eight during the session. Increasing numbers brought increasing wants, without a corresponding increase of contributions towards the maintenance of the school. In less than three months after the opening there had accrued a deficit of $2,300, which the committee had no means of meeting; and it was evident that this deficit would grow with time. The alternative presented was to appeal to the trustees or to abandon the undertaking. The committee were pledged to make no such appeal—all except the President of the college, who had been elected since the committee was appointed, and had been added to it after his election. He volunteered to take upon himself the individual responsibility of laying the matter before the board, which he did, with the result of obtaining relief from the immediate embarrassment, and of subsequently securing the passage of a resolution whereby the trustees undertook to give the school a fair experiment, by providing the means necessary for its support, not only through the current year, but also through the year ensuing—its further permanence to be dependent on the result. During the second year, therefore, appropriations were made for this school in the same manner as for other departments of the institution, and salaries were assigned to the professors.

The unexpected success of this first session encouraged the trustees to enlarge the accommodations of the School, which they did by appropriating $30,000 to fit up for its uses a building 70 by 30 feet in dimensions, on the college grounds, and providing room in the laboratory and drawing academy for seventy-two students. Eighty-nine were, however, admitted, and the new rooms proved to be inadequate. At the close of the second year the experiment was pronounced a success; and other appropriations, amounting to $70,000 in all, were voted for the construction of a new building, the purchase of a complete equipment, and the estimated current expenses of the third year. From this time on the school continued to grow in numbers and in strength. The new building provided for was prepared during the summer of 1865, and was soon found inadequate to accommodate the increased number of students. In the year 1874 a much larger building was erected at a cost of $150,000, and fitted up with every convenience for the purposes of the school.

When the school was first opened, no examination for admission was required. The course was to extend over three years, and two regular courses were open to students. On the satisfactory conclusion of one of these courses, the student was to receive the degree of Engineer of Mines; and at the conclusion of the other, the degree of Bachelor of Philosophy. Students were also, under certain conditions, permitted to take partial courses, which led to no degree. At the beginning of the second year, however, candidates who desired to enter for a degree were required to pass an examination in algebra, geometry and trigonometry. Experience showed that the most of those who entered were not sufficiently well prepared in mathematics, physics, and general chemistry, to prosecute with advantage the subsequent course; and in 1868 a Preparatory Class (which is practically the first year of the school) was established. At the same time the course of study was enlarged, so as to include four parallel courses of study, to which, in the following year, a fifth course was added—so that now the system of instruction includes five parallel courses of study, viz.:

I. Civil Engineering. III. Metallurgy.
II. Mining Engineering. IV. Geology and Natural History.
V. Analytical and Applied Chemistry.

The plan of instruction includes lectures and recitations in the several departments of study; practice in the chemical, mineralogical, blow-pipe and metallurgical laboratories; projects, estimates, and drawings for the establishment of mines, and for the construction of metallurgical and chemical works, reports on mines, industrial establishments, and field geology.

The detail of subjects in the several courses may be seen from the following

SYNOPSIS OF STUDIES.

The studies in the Preparatory and First Years are alike in the five courses.

PREPARATORY YEAR.

Geometry, Algebra, Trigonometry, and Mensuration.

Physics.

Chemistry, Inorganic and Organic—Lectures and recitations.

French.

German.

Drawing—Pen and colored topography ; sketching from plane models and from nature ; water-color landscapes ; use of instruments, and machine drawing.

FIRST YEAR.

Analytical Geometry and Calculus.

Descriptive Geometry—Plane and spherical projections, warped surfaces—Lectures and exercises.

Shades, Shadows, and Perspective—Lectures and exercises.

Stone-Cutting.

Chemistry, Inorganic and Organic—Lectures and recitations.

Stoichiometry—Lectures and blackboard exercises.

Qualitative Analysis—Lectures and laboratory practice.

Crystallography—Lectures and practical exercises.

Blowpipe Analysis, qualitative—Lectures and laboratory practice.

Botany—recent and fossil.

Zoology—recent and fossil.

French.

German.

Drawing—Use of instruments, problems in descriptive geometry. shade, shadows, perspective and stone-cutting.

SUMMER VACATION.

MEMOIR.

I.—COURSE IN CIVIL ENGINEERING.

SECOND YEAR.

Mechanics—Mechanics of solids; mechanics of liquids; mechanics of gases.

Civil Engineering.

Strength of Materials.

Geodesy - Surveying with chain, with compass, with angular instruments, and with plane table; Practical Trigonometry, Levelling, Hydrography, Geodesic operations for the construction of maps.

Quantitative Analysis—Lectures and laboratory practice.

Metallurgy—General processes, fuel, furnaces, iron and steel.

Geology—Lithological, cosmical, physiographic, historic and dynamic.

Mineralogy—Determinative mineralogy, and blowpipe examination of minerals.

Physics—Undulatory theory of light, Ohm's law, etc.

German.

Drawing—Machines, furnaces, and other constructions.

SUMMER VACATION.

MEMOIR.

THIRD YEAR.

Mechanics applied to engineering, problems of hydraulics and pneumatics.

Constructions—Machines, turbines and other water-wheels, air and steam engines, etc.

Economic Geology—Theory of mineral veins; ores; deposits and distribution of metals, iron, copper, lead, etc.; character, history, uses and distribution of coal, lignite, peat, petroleum, salts, clays, building and ornamental stones, fertilizers, etc.

Drawing—Project drawings.

Project—Dissertation and drawings, embracing the solution of some problem in engineering assigned by the Faculty of the School.

II.—COURSE IN MINING ENGINEERING.

SECOND YEAR.

Mechanics—Mechanics of solids; mechanics of liquids; mechanics of gases.

Mining Engineering—Surveying and mining operations.

Strength of Materials.

Quantitative Analysis—Lectures and laboratory practice.

Blowpipe Analysis, quantitative—Lectures and laboratory practice.

Metallurgy—General processes, fuels, furnaces, iron and steel.

Geology—Lithological, cosmical, physiographic, historic and dynamic.

Mineralogy—Determinative mineralogy, and blowpipe examination of minerals.

Physics—Undulatory theory of light, Ohm's law, etc.

German.

Drawing—Machines, plans, etc.

SUMMER VACATION.

MEMOIR.

THIRD YEAR.

Mining Engineering—Mining machines.

Assaying—Lectures and laboratory practice; ores of lead, silver, gold, tin, antimony, copper, nickel, cobalt, and mercury; gold and silver bullion.

Economic Geology—Theory of mineral veins; ores; deposits and distribution of metals, iron, copper, lead, etc.; character, history, uses, and distribution of coal, lignite, peat, petroleum, salt, clay, building and ornamental stones, fertilizers, etc.

Metallurgy—Lectures on copper, lead, silver, gold, zinc, etc.

Quantitative Analysis—Laboratory practice.

Drawing—Project drawings.

Project—Dissertation and drawings, embracing the solution of some mechanical, mining or metallurgical problem, assigned by the Faculty of the School.

DEGREE OF MINING ENGINEER.

III.—COURSE IN METALLURGY.

SECOND YEAR.

Mechanics.

Quantitative Analysis—Lectures and laboratory practice.

Blowpipe Analysis, quantitative—Lectures and laboratory practice.

Metallurgy—General processes, fuels, furnaces, iron and steel.

Geology—Lithological, cosmical, physiographic, historic, and dynamic.

Mineralogy—Determinative mineralogy, and blowpipe examination of minerals.

German.

Drawing—Furnaces, machines, etc.

SUMMER VACATION.

MEMOIR.

THIRD YEAR.

Assaying—Lectures and laboratory practice; ores of lead, silver, gold, tin, antimony, copper, nickel, cobalt, and mercury; and gold and silver bullion.

Economic Geology—Theory of mineral veins; ores; deposits and distribution of metals, iron, copper, lead, etc.; character, history, uses and distribution of coal, lignite, peat, petroleum, salt, clays, building and ornamental stones, fertilizers, etc.

Metallurgy—Lectures on copper, lead, silver, gold, zinc, etc.

Quantitative Analysis—Laboratory practice.

Lithology—The character and genesis of rock masses; microscopic and chemical study of rocks.

Drawing—Project drawings.

Project—Dissertation and drawings, embracing the solution of a metallurgical problem, assigned by the Faculty of the School.

DEGREE OF BACHELOR OF PHILOSOPHY.

IV.—COURSE IN GEOLOGY AND NATURAL HISTORY.

SECOND YEAR.

Quantitative Analysis—Lectures and laboratory practice.

Blowpipe Analysis, quantitative—Lectures and laboratory practice.

Mineralogy—Determinative mineralogy, and blowpipe examination of minerals.

Metallurgy—General processes, fuels, furnaces, iron and steel.

Geology—Lithological, cosmical, physiographic, historic and dynamic.

German.

Drawing—Making sections, sketching and drawing fossils and other natural history objects.

SUMMER VACATION.

MEMOIR.

THIRD YEAR.

Economic Geology—Theory of mineral veins; ores, deposits and distribution; metals, iron, copper, lead, etc.; character, history, uses and distribution of coal, lignite, peat, petroleum, salt, clays, building and ornamental stones, fertilizers, etc.

Lithology—The character and genesis of rock masses; microscopic and chemical study of rocks.

Palæontology—Systematic review of recent and fossil forms of life, animal and vegetable.

Metallurgy.

Drawing—Project drawings.

Dissertation, embracing results of observation and study of some subject, assigned by the Faculty of the School.

DEGREE OF BACHELOR OF PHILOSOPHY.

V.—COURSE IN ANALYTICAL AND APPLIED CHEMISTRY.

SECOND YEAR.

Applied Chemistry—Lectures on chemical manufactures; acids, alkalies, and salts; glass, porcelain, pottery, limes, mortars and cements.

Quantitative Analysis—Lectures and laboratory practice.

Blowpipe Analysis, quantitative—Lectures and laboratory practice.

Mineralogy—Determinative mineralogy and blowpipe examination of minerals.

Metallurgy—General processes, fuels, furnaces, iron and steel.

Geology—Lithological, cosmical, physiographic, historic and dynamic.

German.

Drawing—Furnaces, machines, apparatus, etc.

SUMMER VACATION.

MEMOIR.

THIRD YEAR.

Applied Chemistry—(1) Fuel and its applications; (2) Artificial Illumination: candles, oils, lamps, petroleum, gas and its products; (3) Food and Drink: water, milk, cereals, starch, bread, meats, tea, coffee, sugar, fermentation, wine, beer, spirits, vinegar, preservation of food, tobacco, etc.; (4) Clothing: textile fabrics, bleaching, dyeing, calico printing, paper, tannin, glue, india-rubber, gutta-percha, etc.; (5) Artificial Fertilizers: guano, superphosphates, poudrettes, etc.; (6) Disinfectants, Antiseptics, Preservation of Wood, etc.

Quantitative Analysis—Laboratory practice.

Assaying—Lectures and laboratory practice: ores of lead, silver, gold, tin, antimony, copper, nickel, cobalt, mercury, and gold and silver bullion.

Economic Geology—Theory of mineral veins; deposits of metallic ores: iron, copper, etc.; coal, peat, lignite, petroleum, salt, clay, building and ornamental stones, fertilizers, etc.

Metallurgy—Lectures on copper, lead, silver, gold, zinc, mercury, etc.

Drawing—Project drawings.

Dissertation, embracing results of observations and experimental study on some chemical subject, assigned by the Faculty of the School.

DEGREE OF BACHELOR OF PHILOSOPHY.

The course in the several Departments of Instruction is as follows:

MATHEMATICS.

Preparatory Year.—Geometry, plane volumetric and spherical; algebra, so far as to include the general theory of equatations; trigonometry, plane, analytical and spherical; mensuration of surfaces and of volumes.

First Year.—Analytical geometry of two and three dimensions; differential and integral calculus, with applications to mechanics and astronomy.

PHYSICS.

The students in the preparatory year are occupied during the first term with the subject of Heat, including the Steam-Engine, while the second term is employed in the study of Voltaic Electricity, Magnetism and Electro-magnetism. These courses of Lectures are fully illustrated by appropriate experiments; the instruction is conveyed by lectures and recitations, practical problems being occasionally proposed for solution.

During the second year, courses of lectures are delivered on the laws of Electro-dynamics, on the Mechanical Theory of Heat, on Mathematical Optics, and on the Undulatory Theory of Light. Portions of these courses are accompanied by experimental demonstrations.

The cabinet of Physical Apparatus will rank with the best on this continent, and extensive additions are made to it each year.

MECHANICS.

This subject is taught during the second year. The course of instruction embraces the following subjects:

Representation and measurement of forces; composition, resolution, and equilibrium of forces; principles of moments and virtual moments; theory of parallel forces; application to centre of gravity; stability.

Elementary machines; friction, resistance to rolling, stiffness of cords, atmospheric resistance.

General equations of motion; rectilineal, uniform, and uniformly varied motion; curvilinear motion, free and constrained; centrifugal force; application to the governor; vibratory motion; application to the pendulum; motions of translation and rotation; moment of inertia, principal axes and ellipsoid of inertia; laws of impact; centre of percussion; general theorem of work; accumulation of work; application to fly-wheel.

Mechanics of fluids; pressure due to weight; equal transmission of pressures; application to hydraulic press; buoyancy and flotation; application to specific gravity.

Tension and elasticity of gases and vapors; laws of variation; application to pumps and siphons; investigation of the barometer formula; motion of liquids in pipes and open channels; living force of fluids; application to hydraulic ram; mechanics of capillarity.

PRACTICAL ASTRONOMY.—Students of the second and third years may be admitted to the course of practical astronomy in the observatory, which will include the theory and use of the transit instrument and sextant, and the determination of geographical position. Instruction in this branch is given by the assistant in the observatory.

DRAWING AND GRAPHICS.

During the first session of the preparatory year, the student is taught the use of drawing instruments, and then to execute topographical maps. He is first instructed in the use of the pen to delineate lines of level, shaded with lines of declivity, and completed with the conventional signs of different features, such as water, forests, marshes, cultivated grounds, outcrops of veins, etc. ; subsequently he is taught to represent the same with the application of the conventional signs and colors used by our government and civil engineers. During the second session the course of instruction includes sketching in pencil from plane models, and from nature ; afterwards colored sketches or landscape drawing in water colors, and machine drawing.

During the first year, Descriptive Geometry is taught. The course of instruction includes the study of Davies' treatise on this subject, with lectures and blackboard exercises, illustrated by Olivier's and other models, exposing the more difficult problems of intersections and the generation of warped surfaces.

The instruction in drawing includes the use of mathematical instruments in constructing on paper the problems of Descriptive Geometry.

During the second session Graphics are taught, including the study of Davies, Shades and Shadows and Perspective, and Warren's Stone-cutting, with explanatory lectures, the exhibition of models, and the solution of various problems of shades and shadows.

The course of drawing includes instruction and practice in the use of instruments, the pen and brush, with India-ink, in drawing mathematical forms in projection and perspective, shading them, casting their shadows, and washing them. This is followed by an application of the principles learned to the execution of a drawing of a machine, or the section of a furnace, wherein the shadows are accurately calculated and washed, and the drawing is appropriately colored.

In the second year the course includes, during the first session, the drawing of machines, mills, furnaces, etc., from plane models. These are shaded, their shadows calculated and cast, and the whole properly colored. The dimensions are also quoted, so that these drawings serve as types of working drawings.

During the second session the students draw from various models in relief, chiefly furnaces and machines. They first make a free-hand sketch from the relief, and upon it place the dimensions which they measure; subsequently they draw the finished representation in the academy to a proper scale, with shades, shadows, colors and dimensions. This practice is of benefit in accustoming the student to take rapid sketches of established works upon which he may be required to report, or by which he may wish to direct himself.

CIVIL ENGINEERING

Is taught during the second and third years. In the second year the course of instruction includes Surveying (theory and practice), Topography, Geodesic operations for the tracing of maps, Hydrography, Strength of Materials, etc., followed by a course of instruction in general engineering statics, and a course of roads and bridges, etc., according to Mahan's Civil Engineering, which is used as a text book, with Vinton's Strength of Materials.

The drawing includes maps, problems in stone-cutting, and copies from models, plane and in relief.

In the third year the course consists of lectures on Hydraulics, Pneumatics, and Machines.

During the vacation at the close ot the last year, (1874-75), the first year students were required to prepare a memoir on Cements and Artificial Stones, to be handed in on or before November 1st, 1875.

For graduation, students of the third year were required to execute the following memoir and project:

A Memoir on the Transformation of Movements by Eccentrics—to be handed in on or before November 1st, 1875.

And on or before the 15th of April, 1876, the following

Project for a railroad;

A topographical levelling made by the present graduating class, having given them a system of horizontal lines representing a certain contour, they were required for a project in Civil Engineering to determine a variable grade between two points, following a given line, such that the cuttings and fillings may be as nearly equal as possible, and for a slope or ramp, 5 met. wide, destined for the establishment of an automatic inclined plane by the Mining Engineers.

Upon the grade are to be laid two parallel railroads, each 0·90 met. wide, substantially made. The side slopes shall be two upon three for earth, and two upon one for rock. The cross sections shall be calculated not more than 6 met. apart, and the profile of determined grade and cross sections, as well as actual line of surface, shall be drawn, referred to any horizontal plane. Give also the plan of the road, and the position of the slope stakes, in each section, referring the cuttings and fillings in red to the grade.

In the text the cuttings and fillings between the cross sections must be closely evaluated, the details of the railroad construction described, and some attempt made at estimating the cost of the whole work under conditions of the ground which the student may assume from his knowledge of it.

MINING ENGINEERING.

Mining Engineering is taught during the second and third years. The instruction comprises a course of lectures illustrating the theory and practice of mining operations at home and abroad; giving the general principles of reconnoitering and surveying mineral property and mines; the attack, development, and administration of mines and the mechanical preparation of ores, with the exhibition and use of all necessary reconnoitering and surveying instruments, particularly the mining theodolite, and the exhibition of various models.

In surveying, the student is taught to make surface and subterranean surveys, to direct and adjust his works; also the solution of some problems of underground surveying by descriptive geometry, and many special examples of determining lines on the surface corresponding to given lines below, etc.

Attack describes the miners' method; the use of drills, picks, powder, nitro-glycerine and new explosives, compressed air, etc.; the proper location and construction of tunnels, slopes, shafts, wells for sounding, Artesian wells, salt and oil wells; preceded by a theory and description of the most typical veins, true or irregular, and other deposits of ore, salt, coal and oil, exemplified at home and abroad.

Development includes the description of the best methods in experience of laying out subterranean works for production and conservation in the present and future; for proper and economic ventilation, transportation, hoisting, pumping or draining, distribution of workmen, etc.

Administration includes a review of the foregoing, with regard to a concentration of ideas and a general comparison of production cost to market price of untreated ore.

Here the student is taught to forecast the expense of the establishments he must make; their annual cost; the cost of miners, employees, machines, material, etc.; and offset these with the result of production, so endeavoring to solve the problem of making a given mine pay in given circumstances, by scientific attack, distribution and general rational economy.

Mechanical preparation describes the various accepted methods of reducing massive ore to a condition either yielding metal or fitting the material for metallurgical processes. Models of stamps, crushers, shaking-tables, sluices, etc., are exhibited, with plans and sections of mills, and coal-breakers at home and abroad.

During the vacation at the close of last year

(1874-75), the first year students pursuing the course of Mining Engineering were required to prepare a memoir on Cars and Brakes for Exterior Transportation, to be handed in on or before November 1st, 1875.

For graduation in 1876 in the course of Mining Engineering, third year students were required to execute the following memoir and projects:

A Memoir on Hoisting Machinery, to be handed in on or before November 1st, 1875.

And on or before April 15th, 1876, the following Projects:

I. Metallurgical Project for an establishment to produce annually 30,000 tons of Bessemer steel. The establishment will produce its own Bessemer Pig, but will purchase its Spiegel. The works must be situated at some point in the United States, where the ores and fuel suitable for the manufacture of Bessemer Pig can be had.

II. Mining Project: On a slope such as the Civil Engineering project describes, the Mining Engineers will establish all the apparatus and machinery for an automatic inclined plane. They will draw and describe the landings at both ends, the cars, the cables, the rollers, the pulleys and brakes, method of hitching, etc. The Cabany car of Anzin is preferred; the cars may load 1,000 kils. of coal, the width of railroad being 0·90 metres. The student will determine the dimensions of the car, and, assuming the product of the mine to be constant and indefinite, he will examine what system of trains on the slope in question will effect the transportation of the greatest volume in a given time, between the two given points, admitting plenty of room at the landings for making up trains or for hitching on to an endless chain if one is used.

MACHINES.

The course of machines, which is inseparable from that of mining engineering, is given during the third year. It teaches the theory of the machines used in mining works. It is the application of mechanics to the construction of water-wheels, turbines, wind-mills, steam and heat engines, pumps and ventilators, transmission of force by compressed air, and the formulæ with their theory for the resistance of materials. Models of water-wheels, steam-cylinders, steam-engines, blowing-machines, etc., are exhibited.

In the resistance of materials the calculations are shown for the sections of different parts of machines, the fly-wheel, pump-rods, connecting-rods, etc., also for such constructions as retaining walls, arches, timbering, supports, etc. The course of the third year also includes a plan of drawing and estimates for some projected work of mining, or the construction of a machine for some of the uses of mining. The system ot projects is to the young engineer a real practical application of all his three years' study by which he is made to investigate prices, compare theories, models, methods, and dispositions, and in competing with his class to take pains to furnish the best arguments, illustrations, and calculations he can, in order to support his views.

Among the instruments and models for illustration and use in this department are the following, viz.: a full set of surveying instruments; ore mill and shaft, crushers, stamps, boring derrick, rods and tools, shaking-tables, washing-tables, etc., for mechanical preparation of ores, in solid models; steam engines, sections ot steam cylinders, water-wheels, turbines, in solid models; timber and masonry joints, roof and bridge trusses, masonry canal lock, in solid models; a machine for testing the resistance of materials to transverse, tensile and crushing strains, constructed to apply and accurately weigh strains of from five to fifty thousand pounds; the Olivier models, forming all mathematical surfaces by silk threads, and admitting of a variety of transformations; also other models illustrating general and special problems of Descriptive Geometry, shades and shadows, and stone-cutting; drawings of machines and parts of machines for studying and copying; also, landscapes, in crayon and in water color, for instruction in sketching; models of mining machines and mining tools, stationary steam-engines, single and double cylinders, sections of steam-cylinders, water-wheels, turbines, shaking-tables, stamps, crushers, blowing-machines, pumps, etc.; Derill's apparatus for fusion at high temperatures, with the necessary machinery for the compression of air.

MODERN LANGUAGES.

The design in this department is to teach the students how to read French and German scientific books with facility.

Instruction is given for four hours a week in each of these languages during the preparatory year, and two hours a week during the first year, and in German one hour a week during the second year. As the text books employed in the class-room are altogether works on science, the students can acquire a sufficient vocabulary to enable them to use French and German authors in all the departments of the school.

No attempt is made to produce accomplished scholars in all branches of German and French literature, but attention is concentrated upon the immediate wants of the young men. In this way no time is lost, and the instruction becomes thoroughly practical.

GENERAL CHEMISTRY.

The Preparatory Class attend three exercises a week in General Chemistry throughout the year. It is intended to lay the foundation of a thorough knowledge of the theory of the subject preliminary to the practical instruction in the chemical laboratory. For this purpose the class is drilled upon the lectures, with free use of the best text-books. The students are expected to write out full notes, which must be exhibited to the Professor at the close of each session. At the end of the year the members of the class must pass a rigid examination before they can be admitted to a higher grade.

The first year students also attend three times a week during the year, and receive instruction in Theoretical Chemistry, adapted to the wants of special scientific students. They are expected to keep full notes to be exhibited at the end of the year.

ANALYTICAL CHEMISTRY.

There is a laboratory devoted to Qualitative Analysis, another to Quantitative Analysis, and an Assay laboratory. These laboratories are provided with all the necessary apparatus and fixtures, and each is under the special charge of a competent assistant. Each student is provided with a convenient table with drawers and cupboards, and is supplied with a complete outfit of apparatus and chemical reagents.

During the first year Qualitative Analysis is taught by lectures and black-board exercises, and the student is required to repeat all the experiments at his table in the laboratory. Having acquired a thorough experimental knowledge of the reactions of a group of bases or acids, single members of the group or mixtures are submitted to him for identification. He thus proceeds from simple to complex cases till he is able to determine the composition of the most difficult mixtures. Constant use is made of the spectroscope in these investigations.

When the student shows on written and experimental examination that he is sufficiently familiar with Qualitative Analysis he is allowed to enter the Quantitative laboratory.

During the second and third years, Quantitative Analysis is taught by lectures and blackboard exercises, and the student is required to execute in the laboratory in a satisfactory manner a certain number of analyses. He first analyzes substances of known composition, such as crystallized salts, that the accuracy of his work may be tested by a comparison of his results with the true percentage.

These analyses are repeated till he has acquired sufficient skill to insure accurate results. He is then required to make analyses of more complex substances, such as coals, limestones, ores of copper, iron, zinc, and nickel, pig-iron, slags, technical products, etc., cases in which the accuracy of the work is determined by duplicating the analyses, and by comparing the results of different analysts.

Volumetric methods are employed whenever they are more accurate or more expeditious than the gravimetric methods. In this way each student acquires practical experience in the chemical analyses of the ores and products which he is most likely to meet in practice.

ASSAYING.

During the third year the student is admitted to the Assay laboratory, where he is provided with a suitable table and a set of assay apparatus; and where he has access to crucible and muffle furnaces, and to volumetric apparatus for the assay of alloys of gold and silver.

The general principles, as well as the special methods of assaying, are explained in the lecture-room, and at the same time the ores of the various metals and their appropriate fluxes are exhibited and described.

The student is then supplied with the different ores, and is required to assay each ore in duplicate, under the immediate supervision of the instructor.

To facilitate the assay of ores of the precious metals, a system of weights has been introduced, by which the weight of the silver or gold globule obtained shows at once, without calculation, the number of troy ounces in a ton of ore.

STOICHIOMETRY.

Stoichiometry, the arithmetic of chemistry, is taught in a special course of lectures and blackboard exercises during the second session of the first year; and its practical applications are developed in lectures on quantitative analysis and assaying.

APPLIED CHEMISTRY.

The instruction in Applied Chemistry extends through the second and third years, and consists of lectures, illustrated by experiments, diagrams and specimens.

The subjects discussed are:

I. Chemical manufactures: acids, alkalies and salts.

(1.) Sulphur, sulphurous acid, hyposulphites, sulphuric acid, bisulphide of carbon, etc.

(2.) Common salt, soda ash, hydrochloric acid, chlorine, binoxide of manganese, bleaching powder, chlorates, chlorimetry, etc.

(3.) Carbonate of potash, caustic potash, alkalimetry, acidimetry, etc.

(4.) Iodine, bromine, etc.

(5.) Sodium, aluminium, magnesium.

(6.) Phosphorus, matches, etc.

(7.) Nitrates of potash and soda, gunpowder, gun-cotton, nitro-glycerine, etc.

(8.) Ammonia salts.

(9.) Cyanides.

(10.) Alum, copperas, blue vitriol, salts of magnesia, baryta, strontia, etc.

(11.) Borates, stannates, tungstates, chromates, etc.

(12.) Mercury salts, silver salts, photography.

(13.) Electro-metallurgy.

(14.) Oils, fats, soaps, glycerine.

(15.) Pigments, paints, essential oils, resins, varnishes, inks.

II. Glass, porcelain, and pottery.

III. Limes, mortars, hydraulic cements, gypsum, lutes, putty, etc.

IV. Fuel and its applications.

V. Artificial illumination: candles, oils, and lamps, petroleum, gas and its products.

VI. Food and drink: water, milk, cereals, starch, bread, meat, tea, coffee, sugar; fermentation, wine, beer, spirits, vinegar, preservation of food, tobacco, etc.

VII. Clothing: textile fabrics, bleaching, dyeing, calico printing, paper, tanning, glue, india-rubber, gutta percha, etc.

VIII. Fertilizers: guano, superphosphates, poudrettes, etc.

XI. Disinfectants, antiseptics, preservation of wood, etc.

The second year students of 1875–76, in the course in Analytical and Applied Chemistry, were required to hand in on or before November 1st, 1875—

A Memoir on one of the following subjects: (1.) On a Rational Classification of Organic Compounds. (2.) On the Decompositions and Transformations of Organic Compounds. (3.) On the Additive and Substitution Products of Benzole. (C_6H_6). The third year students in the same course were required to hand in—

A Memoir on one of the following subjects: (1.) Milk, Butter and Cheese. (2.) Fermentation, Wine, Beer, and Spirits. (3.) Dyeing and Calico Printing. (4.) India-rubber and Gutta Percha;

And the following:

Chemical Dissertation on a subject which they may select, subject to the approval of the President and the Professors of General Chemistry and Analytical Chemistry.

COLLECTION ILLUSTRATING APPLIED CHEMISTRY.

Several thousand specimens of materials and products illustrating all the subjects included in the course of instruction in Applied Chemistry are arranged in a cabinet of industrial chemistry for the illustration of the lectures and inspection of the students.

The collection includes suites of materials, the products of the various operations, and diagrams of machinery and apparatus. Specially rich are the collections illustrating common salt, aluminium, phosphorus, matches, sulphur and sulphuric acid, photography, photo-relief printing, photo-lithography, electro-metallurgy, petroleum, coal gas, coal tar and its products, pigments, dyeing and calico printing, tanning, glue, india-rubber, beet and cane sugar, ceramics, glass, fertilizers, disinfectants, etc.

GEOLOGY AND PALÆONTOLOGY.

FIRST YEAR.

Botany and Zoölogy, as an introduction to Palæontology—lectures and conferences throughout the year.

During the vacation at the close of the first year, students pursuing the course in Geology and Natural History are required to prepare a memoir on one of the following subjects, to be handed in on or before November 1st:

(1.) Notes on the Flora or Fauna of any Geographical District visited. (2.) Observations on the structure, distribution, and habits of any of our fresh water fishes. (3.)

Catalogues and collections of mollusks inhabiting any lakes, rivers, or districts. (4.) Notes on the economy of the observed insects. (5.) Notes on the various observed methods by which the seeds of plants are distributed.

SECOND YEAR.

Lithology: Minerals which form rocks and rock masses of the different classes—lectures and practical exercises.

Geology—Cosmical, Physiographic and Historical—lectures throughout the year.

During the vacation at the close of the second year, students pursuing the course of Geology and Natural History are required to prepare a memoir on one of the following subjects, to be handed in on or before November 1st:

(1.) Report on the Geology of any district visited, embracing: *a.* Topographical features and their cause. *b.* Surface Geology. *c.* Sections of Strata with lithological character, thickness, dip, strike, and fossils of each bed. Sketches of rock outcrops. *d.* Suit of specimens of rocks and fossils, rocks 3 x 4 x 1 inches.

(2.) Report on any special formation which may be examined, embracing: *a.* The geographical area of its outcrops. *b.* Its mineral character, and origin of the material composing it. *c.* List and collection of its fossils. *d.* Reading of the history of its deposition.

(3.) Report on any examined deposit of ores or other useful minerals: as, *a.* The magnetic iron ores of New York and New Jersey, phenomena and history. *b.* The limonite ores of the Alleghany belt, character of deposits and age. *c*. The zinc ores of Franklin or Friedensville. *d*. The chromic iron of the Alleghany belt, where and how it occurs.

THIRD YEAR.

Economic Geology: Theory of Mineral Veins; Ores, Deposits and Distribution of Iron, Copper, Lead, Zinc, Gold, Silver, Mercury and other metals; Graphite, Coal, Lignite, Peat, Asphalt, Petroleum, Salt, Clay, Limestone, Cements, Building and Ornamental Stones, Gems, Fertilizers, etc.

Palæontology: Systematic review of recent and fossil forms of life—lectures throughout the year.

For graduation in the course of Geology and Natural History, students will be required to present, on or before the 15th of April, a dissertation on one of the following subjects:

(1.) The mesozoic sandstones of New Jersey and the Connecticut Valley, their geological phenomena, history and relations to the associated trap rocks.

(2.) The limonite iron ores of the Alleghany belt; their phenomena, age, and origin—*i. e.*, where and how they occur; when and how they were deposited.

(3.) Eozoon Canadense; is it organic?

The rooms occupied by these departments are a museum 100 x 28 feet, a lecture room 30 x 40 feet, a conference room 22 x 32 feet, and a laboratory and professor's study, each 22 x 16 feet.

The Geological Hall is provided with wall and table cases along the sides, and the centre is occupied by a series of casts and skeletons of the larger vertebrates.

The table cases in the Geological Hall form closed cabinets below, in which there are over 700 numbered drawers or trays, each 3 x 1½ feet in area. These trays contain special suites of specimens, and more than half the entire geological collection.

The collections in this hall embrace:

1st. A lithological collection of 500 specimens of rocks, and the minerals that make rocks.

2nd. A collection illustrating Historical Geology, in which the rocks and characteristic fossils of all the different formations are arranged in such order as to represent the geological column. This collection numbers about 25,000 specimens.

3rd. A collection of ores, coals, oils, clays, and building materials, and other useful minerals illustrative of the course of lectures on Economic Geology, and believed to give the fullest representation of the mineral resources of the United States of any collection yet made.

4th. A Palæontological series, which includes collections of recent and fossil vertebrates, articulates, mollusks, radiates, and plants. In this series is to be found the largest collection of fossil plants belonging to any institution in the world, including many remarkably large and fine specimens, and over 200 new species, of which representatives are not known to exist elsewhere. Also the most extensive series of fossil fishes in the country, including, among many new and remarkable forms, the only specimens known of the gigantic *Dinichthys ;* a suite of Ward's casts of extinct saurians and mammals ; a fine skeleton of the great Irish elk, etc., etc.

MINERALOGY.

The studies of the department of Mineralogy continue through two years. In the first year the students are instructed in crystallography and in the use of the blow-pipe. Lectures on crystallography embrace the entire subject, including the description of both normal and distorted forms, in the study of which the students have access to a collection of more than three hundred models, embracing all the possible and theoretical forms. Besides this collection, they have the use of a collection of 150 glass models ; in addition to these two collections, most of the species in the collection of minerals are illustrated by models in wood of nearly all the forms.

The exercises in qualitative blow-piping last through half of the year, and are composed of the analysis of mixtures of alloys and minerals. In the examination the students are required to examine one substance containing from five to six elements, one containing eight, and one containing twelve different elements. The collection of blow-pipe substances is contained in 400 different bottles.

The blow-pipe laboratory is a large, well ventilated room, to which the students have access at all hours of the day, where each student has a drawer with a lock assigned to him, which he retains until the close of the term.

In the second year the lectures are illustrated with a very complete lantern, arranged for the electric and lime light, presented by F. A. Schermerhorn. Conferences are held at least once a week, where the students are required to determine minerals placed before them, by the eye, or by asking questions with regard to their characters which could not be determined without experiment. They are required to give the name, composition, crystalline form, and prominent blow-pipe and physical characteristics of every mineral they determine. To facilitate this work, they have a collection of about 2,000 carefully-labelled specimens, to which they have free access, and on which they are allowed to try the usual physical and blow-pipe experiments.

They have, besides, constant access to the cabinet of minerals, which contains fifteen thousand specimens, arranged in table cases, intended to show the different characteristics of minerals, and about two thousand arranged in wall cases to show their associations.

The lectures on mineralogy comprise descriptive mineralogy, properly speaking, and physical and optical mineralogy in all its departments; for which purpose the cabinets contain 150 sections of minerals cut perpendicular to their axes, and 25 or 30 sections of chemical compounds, a series of 12 prisms to illustrate the property of dichroism, and a dichroscope for the purpose of studying them. For the study of sections, the laboratory has a Groth polariscope; for the study of the phenomena of parallel and divergent light, and also for measuring the optical axes, a Soliel polariscope, a Wheatstone Neuremburg apparatus, presented by D. Willis James; De Lenormont's apparatus with sections for the study of the conductibility of heat in minerals has been provided for the use of the laboratory; a Fouques magneto-electric apparatus for the analysis of rocks; Derill's apparatus for fusion at high temperatures, with the necessary machinery for the compression of air; a Ross microscope for the study of rocks by polarized light, with the analyzer and polarizer arranged so as to be thrown in and out of the field at will without disturbing the instrument; a Jolly's balance for specific gravity. There are besides these a fine Wollaston goniometer, by Deluil, of Paris, presented by the late Gouverneur Kemble; a Mitscherlich goniometer, presented by Dr. C. R. Agnew; and a Babinet's goniometer, presented by D. Willis James; besides Carrangeau's application goniometer. For the measurement of angles and the indices of refraction, there are seventeen glass prisms of different composition and angles, and four quartz prisms cut in different directions with regard to the axes. All of these different pieces of apparatus are illustrated by apparatus adapted to the lantern. The lantern polariscope has two Nicols prisms, which are $2\frac{3}{4}$ inches on a side, a saccharometer, a dichroscope; a megascope, and microscope arranged for projecting the phenomena of minerals and rocks under polarized light.

The vertical lantern is arranged for the study of polarization of liquids, &c. All of this lantern apparatus was presented by S. L. M. Barlow.

The collection of minerals was founded by a valuable collection, given as the first donation to the school by the late George T. Strong, of this City, which was very shortly supplemented by the donation of another collection by the late

Gouverneur Kemble, containing many autographs and specimens from the cabinet of Hany. As these collections were both very rich in duplicates, very many valuable additions have been made to the cabinet by exchange. Collections were also made in Europe during several years, and were presented to the school through the generosity of the late John Caswell, W. H. Aspinwall, R. P. Parrott, Morris K. Jessup, D. S. Egleston, W. E. Dodge, Jr., C. Lanier, and J. Crearer. The crystals in this collection are arranged upon pedestals in such a way that they can be readily seen and examined by the student. For the expenses of this department, and for the increase of the collections of instruments and minerals, the trustees make an annual appropriation of five hundred dollars.

METALLURGY.

The course in metallurgy embraces lectures upon combustion, construction of furnaces, preparations of fuels, and the metallurgy of cast iron, steel, and all the metals. They last during a period of two years, and discuss all the best methods used in this country and in Europe for extracting metals from the ores, as well as those which may be used in special cases. It is designed to make them as practical as possible, and for this purpose the economical details of cost are given, when they can be obtained from authentic sources. Special details are given of the ores of this country which are difficult to treat, and to the solution of practical problems which may occur, and to changes which different economic relations are liable to cause in the treatment of the same ore in different localities. More than one thousand photographic negatives, for use in the lantern, have been prepared to illustrate all the principal processes used in modern metallurgical works, as well as the erection and construction of furnaces, blast engines, and other machinery used in metallurgical operations.

The collection illustrating metallurgy includes models of furnaces, and a very large collection of drawings, and tracings in most cases from drawings from which works have actually been built. This collection, which embraces several hundred tracings, has been collected in this country and Europe from the best types of works, and are generally sufficiently detailed to be used as construction drawings. The metallurgical collection, properly speaking, embraces about three thousand specimens, illustrating nearly all the prominent metallurgical processes in every stage of their progress. Many of these specimens have been analyzed and assayed ; and these are constantly open in the museum to the inspection of the students.

As an application of the lectures, the students are required to work out a project and to present working drawings and estimates for the erection of works to treat a given ore in stated conditions, these being generally the problems which require solution in some parts of the United States. Every other year is devoted to projects on iron or steel, the intermediate year being given up to gold, silver, copper, and the other metals. For the expenses and collections of this Department the Trustees appropriate $500 annually.

The metallurgical laboratory connected with this department is provided with all the apparatus for ordinary chemical analysis, and with balances, and embraces a series of three rooms arranged in a building constructed in the year 1874 for the purpose. It is provided with the Bunsen, Orsat, Doyere and Regnault apparatus for the analysis of gases, and Godwin's apparatus for determining their density. It has a vertical spectroscope by Dubosey, and a horizontal one with two prisms, also by Dubosey, the gift of D. Willis James, of this city, and also with Siemen's electric and water pyrometer for the measurement of high temperatures. For the expenses of the Laboratory the Trustees appropriate $250 annually.

In the second year the lectures in metallurgy are supplemented by a course in quantitative blowpiping, where the students are taught to assay gold, silver, lead, copper, bismuth, tin, cobalt, nickel, and coal, for which purpose a blowpipe laboratory is provided with ten balances of exceedingly delicate construction, made by Lingke of Freiburg. The examination in this department consists in the assays of ores the values of which are determined within a limited time. The students are taught both the use of the balances and of Harcourt's scale, as well as the use of the micrometer for measuring buttons.

VACATION WORK.

MEMOIR.

During the vacations, at the close of the first and second years, students are required to prepare memoirs on subjects assigned to them by the Faculty.

These memoirs must be based upon the personal examination of works in actual operation, must be illustrated by drawings made to scale, and accompanied, when possible, by specimens. Mention must be made of works visited and books consulted.

The memoirs are bound into volumes for preservation at the School.

The following subjects for memoirs were assigned for the vacation of 1875:

FOR STUDENTS WHO HAD COMPLETED THE FIRST YEAR.

1. Those pursuing the course in Civil Engineering: Cements and Artificial Stones.

2. Those pursuing the course in Mining Engineering: Cars and Brakes for Exterior Transportation.

3. Those pursuing the course in Metallurgy, one of the following subjects: On a rational classification of Organic Compounds; on the decompositions and transformations of Organic Compounds; on the additive and substitution products of Benzole.

4. Those pursuing the course in Geology and Natural History, one of the following:

(1.) Notes on the Flora or Fauna of any geographical district visited. (2.) Observations on the structure, distribution, and habits of any of our fresh water fishes. (3.) Catalogues and collections of Mollusks inhabiting any lakes, rivers or districts, (4.) Notes on the economy of observed insects. (5.) Notes on the various observed methods by which the seeds of plants are distributed.

5. Those pursuing the course in Analytical and Applied Chemistry, one of the following: On a rational classification of Organic Compounds; on the decompositions and transformations of Organic Compounds; on the additive and substitution products of Benzole.

FOR STUDENTS WHO HAD COMPLETED THE SECOND YEAR.

1. Those pursuing the course in Civil Engineering: Transformation of Movements by Eccentrics.

2. Those pursuing the course in Mining Engineering: Hoisting Machinery.

3. Those pursuing the course in Metallurgy, one of the following: (1.) Regenerative Furnaces. (2.) Blair's Direct Process. (3.) The Siemens-Martin's Process.

4. Those pursuing the course in Geology and Natural History, one of the following:

(1.) Report on Geology of any district visited. Embracing: *a.* Topographical features and their cause. *b.* Surface Geology. *c.* Sections of Strata with lithological character, thickness, dip, strike, and fossils of each bed. Sketches of rock outcrops. *d.* Suite of specimens of rocks and fossils, rocks 3 x 4 x 1 inches.

(2.) Report on any special formation which may be examined. Embracing: *a.* The geographical area of its outcrops. *b.* Its mineral character and origin of the material comprising it. *c.* Sets and collections of its fossils. *d.* Reading of the history of its deposition.

(3.) Report on any examined deposits of ores or any other useful minerals: as, *a.* The Magnetic Iron ores of New York and New Jersey, phenomena and history. *b.* The Limonite ores of the Alleghany Belt, character of deposits and age. *c.* The Zinc ores of Franklin or Friedensville. *d.* The Chromic Iron of the Alleghany Belt, where and how it occurs.

Those pursuing the course in Analytical and Applied

Chemistry, one of the following: (1.) Milk, Butter, and Cheese. (2.) Fermentation, Wine, Beer, and Spirits. (3.) Dyeing and Calico Printing. (4.) India-Rubber and Gutta Percha.

During the session, the students may visit the different machine-shops and metallurgical establishments of the city and its environs.

During the vacation, each student is expected to visit mines, metallurgical and chemical establishments, and to hand in on his return a memoir on some subject assigned him. He is also required to bring collections, illustrating his memoir, which collections are placed in the museum, reserved as a medium of exchange, or made use of in the laboratories.

A special Scientific Library has been provided for the use of the students of the School, which already numbers more than six thousand volumes, and is rapidly increasing.

DEGREES.

Those who complete the required course of studies will receive the degree of Engineer of Mines, Civil Engineer, or Bachelor of Philosophy.

Graduates of the School who pursue for one year a course of study prescribed by the Faculty, and present an acceptable dissertation embodying their results, receive the degree of Doctor of Philosophy.

The following statistical table will exhibit the progress of the school:

Year.	No. attending Full Course.	No. of Special Students.	Total.
1864-65	—	—	48
1865-66	—	—	92
1866-67	74	47	121
1867-68	70	52	122
1868-69	62	29	91
1869-70	51	26	77
1870-71	40	57	97
1871-72	57	59	116
1872-73	105	41	146
1873-74	141	27	168
1874-75	180	22	202
1875-76	200	22	222

A writer in the *North American Review*, for January, 1871, in an article on "Mining Schools in the United States," says, with reference to this school:

"The construction of a school building and the provision of apparatus are very far from being all the work accomplished in the six years' life of this institution. The literature of the mining profession in the English language is very imperfect, and it was impossible to conduct the school in any other way than by lectures. These lectures, too, had to be very different from those delivered in

German schools. There the professor not infrequently delivers a loose, often rambling, often too dry, often too agreeable lecture, the object of which, in ordinary cases, is merely to point out to the pupil what direction he should give to his studies. He is expected to go home, and, with the lecture as his guide, to pore over his books, obtaining his real information from them. The cases where the lectures of the professor are expected to be the only or principal source of knowledge are comparatively rare. Here it is very different. The lectures are sometimes all the student has. They must, therefore, be very full in fact, but also well condensed in language, or the course would become interminable. This necessity is far from being a disadvantage. The lectures delivered in New York have the value of original examinations into the sciences they discuss; and when they are published, as is to be hoped they will be in good time, the body of mining science, as contained in American text books, will be very different from that possessed by any other country.

"I have spoken above of the immense labor required to carry on a mining school, and the heterogeneous character of its operations. Of this the school under discussion is a good example. Where there was not a specimen, a crucible, or a furnace, six years have sufficed for the collection of seventy-five thousand specimens, illustrating geology, mineralogy and metallurgy; of models of furnaces, machines, crystals, geometrical sections; of a library of three thousand volumes; of laboratories for assay and for chemical operations, which are larger and better than those of any other mining school in the world. The value of all these must be close on two hundred thousand dollars, and the work has been enormous. Nor can a good school be established with less labor or less expense. But the results are commensurably great. Among all the most famous schools in the world, there is not one so well supplied with apparatus, and not one where all the departments are carried on with the same equal care. Remarkable as it may seem, no school in Europe—unless that in St. Petersburg is to be excepted—can compare with this in the appointments either of its chemical or its assay laboratories.

"If the other schools which are to be founded in this country are established with equal care, fifty years will see a great change for the better in American mines. The enormous losses which are to-day experienced, even in the best conducted works, and the absurdities which are perpetrated in the name of mining, will pass away with the ignorance that causes them."

School of Medicine—Columbia College.

In 1767, the Governors of the college established a Medical School, which continued in existence till November, 1813, at which time the Trustees agreed to incorporate it with the College of Physicians and Surgeons. There was no Faculty of Medicine in the college from 1813 to 1860. In this latter year it was revived by the adoption of the College of Physicians and Surgeons as the Medical Department of the college. The following is a brief historical sketch of the College of Physicians and Surgeons:

The college was chartered March 12th, 1807, by the Regents of the University of the State of New York, pursuant to an act of the Legislature, passed March 24, 1791. The officers were elected May 5, 1807; and the first course of lectures, commencing November 7th, of the same year, were delivered in a small two-story building in Robinson Street. About the close of the session, however, the college, having received from the Legislature an endowment of twenty thousand dollars, was enabled to purchase an edifice in Pearl Street better adapted for their purposes, which was formally opened for the reception of students in November, 1808.

The Medical Department of Columbia College having been discontinued in November, 1813, the union of the two schools, as recommended by the Regents of the University as far back as April 1st, 1811, was, at length, consummated March 7th, 1814, and a commodiously-arranged brick building on the north side of Barclay Street, near Broadway, secured for the new organization.

This alliance, however, proved to be of but short duration, since some of the Faculty withdrew, and, under the authority of Queen's College, New Jersey, established the "New Medical Institution" in a large building in Duane Street. This latter school suspended in 1816.

At this crisis in its affairs, the Regents of the University reorganized the college under an entirely new charter, which gave its management to a Board of twenty-five Trustees, whose tenure of office was subject to the will of the Regents themselves.

In February, 1821, to the dissensions between the college and the New York County Medical Society, which began sometime during 1819, there succeeded new causes of discord between the Trustees and the Faculty. These culminated in the resignation of the entire Faculty in April,

1826, and the appointment of a new corps of Professors a few months afterwards.

The original Faculty, soon after their resignation, revived the Medical Institution, under the auspices of Rutgers (formerly Queen's) College, New Brunswick, New Jersey; but, by legislative enactment, the diplomas were afterwards rendered so manifestly illegal that the Faculty abandoned the contest, and the school ceased to exist.

By a new provision in the Constitution, the Faculty were henceforth excluded from seats in the Board of Trustees, which was now to be composed of a majority of gentlemen who did not belong to the medical profession. As a result, both bodies have since worked in unison for the common good.

The college removed from Barclay to Crosby Street in November, 1837, where its sessions were held up to the inauguration of the present edifice (Fourth Avenue, corner of Twenty-third Street), January 22d, 1856.

Since then nothing noteworthy in its history occurred until the Legislature, by an amendment of its charter, March 24th, 1860, delegated the authority of the Regents to the Trustees; and, in June of this year, also, the institution was constituted the Medical Department of Columbia College, and now bears the title of the "College of

Physicians and Surgeons in the City of New York—Medical Department of Columbia College."

The union is complete in the single respect that the united authority of the two institutions is necessary to the conferring of degrees, all the diplomas bearing the signature of the President of Columbia College, with those of the Faculty of Medicine. The School has an independent Board of Trustees, and its financial affairs are entirely distinct from those of Columbia College.

The following table will show the number of students in attendance since the adoption of the College of Physicians and Surgeons as the Medical Department of the college:

Year.	Number in attendance.	Year.	Number in attendance.
1860–61	260	1868–69	309
1861–62	209	1869–70	338
1862–63	254	1870–71	327
1863–64	288	1871–72	332
1864–65	440	1872–73	359
1865–66	465	1873–74	387
1866–67	344	1874–75	452
1867–68	319	1875–76	410

Libraries.

The College Library is by no means extensive, but remarkably choice, as the merest glance of an instructed eye may readily perceive. It has been repeatedly sifted and arranged, so that, by donations and exchanges, few duplicates remain. It now amounts to upwards of 18,000 volumes, with some 2,500 unbound pamphlets. Its character is, for the most part, scholastic, almost strictly a College Library; not a popular town library for general circulation. Hence, it is deficient in modern and current works of entertainment, and, necessarily, must exclude some specialties absolutely essential to the attractiveness of a general library.

The books in the Library are arranged in ten alcoves, and as many cases with glass doors. Portraits of all the past Presidents of the college—eight in number—that of the second Dr. Johnson, by Trumbull or Stuart—of the Provost, Dr. J. M. Mason, of all the earlier Professors—the head of Dr. Cochrane, by Trumbull, of De Witt Clinton, with a fine head of Columbus, a copy from Parmigiano, compose the gallery of the college. The original *iron crown*, which surmounted the cupola of the old college (King's College) in the days of royalty, now quietly reposes on a bracket.

The history of the Library of Columbia College begins almost contemporaneously with that of the college. Within a few years after the Royal Charter passed the seals, on the 31st of October, 1754, two valuable gifts, together with many important works, given by the Earl of Bute and other individuals, and from the University of Oxford a copy of every work printed at the university press, are recorded by Dr. Moore, in his history of the college, as laying the foundation of the present collection. The gifts just mentioned were the libraries of Mr. Joseph Murray, of the Inner Temple, and of the Rev. Dr. Bristowe, (to the extent of some 1,500 volumes, of which few can now be identified,) whose book-marks occur in some old law works, theological treatises, and other ponderous literature, generally in the form of massive folios. Many, if not most, of the rare old tomes forming these collections were dispersed during the war—from 1776 to '84—when the college was closed as an academic retreat and used as an hospital for the soldiery. In April, 1792, a large addition was made to the college Library in consequence of a grant from the Legislature. In 1811, 1,500 dollars were appropriated by the Board of Trustees, for the purchase of books.

Upon the death of Dr. Kemp, "on the 25th of Nov., 1812, after having for eight and twenty years discharged with great ability and fidelity the duties of Professor of Mathematics and Natural Philosophy," the Trustees bought his library. In 1825, the Trustees bought the collection of Professor da Ponte, consisting of Italian poets, historians, political economists, and miscellaneous literature. In 1836, "the Trustees appropriated 10,000 dollars for the purchase of additional apparatus as well as for adding to the Library the requisite books of reference and illustration." In 1838, "the Trustees made a valuable addition to the College Library, by purchasing that of their former Professor, Dr. N. F. Moore." This collection of an accomplished scholar was especially rich in the classical department and that of Philology; and in Italian literature, embracing many excellent and some beautiful editions.

In 1843 a Professorship of the German Language was established on an endowment of Mr. Gebhard, and a sufficient sum was set apart for the purchase, by Dr. Tellkampf, who occupied the Chair, of a select collection of the standard German authors.

Professor Drisler, during his visit to Europe, 1859–60, was empowered by the Library Committee to purchase works in his department which cover a wide range (among these may be named Canina's great work on the Monuments of Ancient Rome; the new Paris edition of Stephani Thesaurus Græcus; Ritter's Erdkunde, 22 vols.; Histoire de l'Académie des Inscriptions et de Belles-Lettres, 50 vols.; and the Bonn edition of the Byzantine Historians, 48 vols.), chiefly works by German scholars in the sections of Classical Literature and Archæology, Topography, and Mythology, and, in a word, of the various topics that are included in the very wide province of Classical Literature "and the connected subjects."

The Trustees have also enriched the departments of Early English Literature and Belles-Lettres by the purchase, quite recently, of 455 volumes, largely first editions, from their former librarian, Wm. A. Jones, Esq.

Since the removal, in 1857, of the college to its present site, in 49th street, the appropriations have been much more liberal—and have been expended by the late librarian, and his present worthy successor, in a spirit and with a discrimination that, it is trusted, will yield a rich return during the second century of the college.

The library has also been greatly fostered by the generous donations of her early friends, her trustees in their individual capacity, her officers, and her alumni. Among the most prominent instances may be named Dr. John Watts, who gave some of the more valuable of the elder English classics; Robt. Watts, Esq.; Myles Cooper, the second President; Dr. John M. Mason, the Provost, whose name is occasionally found in rare editions of the Greek and Latin classical authors; Dr. Hosack, Senr., who gave a large body of Transactions of learned Societies and Scientific Journals; Dr. Wright Post; Dr. DeKay; John Wells, Esq.; Gen. Laight; Gulian C. Verplanck, Esq.; Messrs. F. Van Rensselaer and De Rham, the personal friends and family connections of Ex-Pres. Moore; Bishop Wainwright; Pres. Duer; W. H. Harison Esq.; Dr. Bowring, of a set of Bentham's works; Washington Irving, of a set of his own writings, more read by the students than the works of any other single author; a number of others to 1851, the most valuable of which are the munificent gift of the British Government of the Public Records of Great Britain, and several most valuable among the "exchanges" of Mons. Vattemare.

Donations amounting to several hundred volumes have been received from the libraries of Messrs. John Anthon and G. T. Strong, and from Mr. Jehiel Post, Prof. Drisler, and Mr. Lenox; and, just previous to the removal of the college, from Dr. Hosack, Jr., and Dr. J. W. Francis, the books originally belonging to the N. Y. Literary and Scientific Society. In 1859, Mr. Johnson, of Stratford, Conn., presented the law library of his father, the first President of Columbia College. This library has now been removed to the Law School of the college (see Law Library), as well as the Law Library of John Jay, the first Chief-Justice of the United States, a gift from his grandson, Mr. John Jay, of this city. In 1872, Bishop Eastburn, of the Class of 1817, left to the college a portion of his library, amounting to 647 volumes of theological and general literature; and finally, Messrs. R. L. and A. Stuart of this city presented a complete set of Clark's collection of the Ante-Nicene Fathers, in 24 volumes. Both the State and general Governments send regularly all their publications, historical and scientific documents.

In continuation of this sketch of the formation of the library, it may be well to name a few of the more prominent works, but this can be done only in the most cursory way. There are valuable editions of the sacred Scriptures, in whole or in part, in more than twenty languages; a fine copy of the *Mischna*, 3 vols. folio, Amsterdam; Kennicott and Houbigant's *Hebrew Bibles;* Bryan Walton's *Biblia Polyglotta*, the *Republican* edition, 1657, so called from its dedication to Cromwell; a fine copy of the *Vulgate*, 3 vols., folio, Paris,

1628; the Codex Friderico-Augustanus, ed. Tischendorf, and the Codex Vaticanus, ed. Vercellone et Cozza, Rome, 5 vols., 4to; *Critici Sacri* —a massive body of biblical criticism.

The Greek and Latin Fathers are well represented in early editions and stately folios—"huge armfuls," as Lamb styled his old English favorites; a phalanx of scholars, orators, saints, and philosophers. Among these, the celebrated edition of St. Chrysostom, by Sir Henry Saville, and the elegant folio edition of 1638 of Cyril of Alexandria. There are rare and choice copies of Lactantius and Tertullian, both Aldines.

A solid array of ecclesiastical historians of the Anglican and Roman Churches is here found. To these may be added "*Conciliorum omnium generalium et provincialium Collectio Regia*," elephant folio, on large paper of admirable texture and marvellous typography, in 38 vols. folio, 1644; comprehending from St. Peter, A.D. 34 to *sedes Vacans*, 1314; from the Council of Ravenna, after the death of Clement V., to the election of John XXI. or XXII.

In this department or section of the library are the original quartos and folios of most of the great Fathers of the Church of England, of the sixteenth and seventeenth centuries: Andrews, Cudworth, Chillingworth, Donne, Heylin, Hammond,

Jewel, Latimer, Leslie, Lightfoot, Bramhall, Fuller, Hall, Mede, Stillingfleet, Wilkins, and modern reprints of Taylor, Barrow, South, Sherlock, Horsley, Jortin, Lowth, Paley. The collection of works on the Evidences includes the sterling writers in that department: Grotius, Paley, Butler, Morgan, E. Smith, Ray, Derham, Jones, Burton, Magee, the Boyle Lectures, the Bridgewater Treatises, with the scarce *Ninth Fragment* of Babbage, down to the present day, along with many rare and curious tracts and treatises, polemical and devotional, principally of the 17th century.

The library is furnished, as a matter of course, with the complete works of the great old masters, as well in Science as in Literature and Speculative Philosophy. The masterpieces left us by the *ancients* in Science are included in the classical portion of the library; among the moderns are Gassendi, Descartes, Newton, Boyle, Leibnitz, and their great compeers. In the different subdivisions of the Sciences, we may quote a few names: as in *Pure Mathematics*, besides the great names just mentioned, Maseres, Sanderson, Carnot, Wolf, Maupertius, Bezout, Bossut, Euler, Clairaut, Bourdon, Dechale, Schottius, Legendre, Lardner, Babbage, Playfair, Hutton, Airy, Monge, Dupin, Walton, Peacock, Sir William Hamilton, Hirsch, Todhunter, etc.

In *Astronomy*, Galileo, Kepler (new ed.), Laplace, Boscovich, Lalande, Bailly, Huygens, Borda, Flamsteed, Delambre, Leverrier, Hansen, Bessel, Brunnow, Argelander, Encke, Oluffsen, Pontecoulant, Struve, Weisse, Gauss, Airy, Chambers, Arago.

In *Physics*, we may mention, among others, English and French, Hutton, Haüy, Libes, Cavallo, Mussenbröck, Noad, Desaguliers, Rutherford, Hooper, Rumford, Nicholson, Muller, Peclet, Poisson, Priestley, Humboldt, Airy, Lockyer, Maxwell, Moigno, Thomson, Tait.

In *Mechanics*, and the applications of mechanics and mathematics to *Engineering*. the *Steam Engine*, etc., there are found some of the best modern treatises.

Among the curiosities of *Old Science*, we should not forget Athanasius Kircher on Optics, and Otto Guericke, with the curious plates, Cornelius Agrippa, Oughtred's Clavis Mathematica, Licetus de Cometis, Borellius de vi percussionis et de motu animalium.

For the departments of Science generally, Chemistry, Natural History, see the Library of School of Science, and for Botany the Botanical Library. There is a good edition of Wilson, and a fine (subscription) copy of Audubon.

In the department of *Literary and Critical Jour-*

nals, the library has full sets—*original editions*—of the Edinburgh, the London Quarterly, the Foreign Quarterly, the Retrospective, the Westminster, North British, the North American, the American Quarterly, and the New York Reviews; Blackwood's, Fraser's and Macmillan's magazines; Rheinisches Museum, Schneidewin's Philologus, Kuhn's Zeitschrift für Vergleichende Sprachforschung; Valpy's Classical Journal, Transactions of the Philological Society, Oxford and Cambridge Essays, Portfolio, Literary World, Notes and Queries.

Of *Dictionaries and Cyclopedias*, connecting the departments of History and Biography, and the worlds of Literature and Science, there are the works of Bayle, Moreri, Chambers; D'Herbelot's Bibliotheque Orientale, Biographie Universelle, Chalmers' and Rose's Biographical Dictionaries, and the Nouvelle Biographie Moderne, the Encyclopedia of Diderot and D'Alembert, the Britannica, third and eighth (last) editions, the Metropolitana, the Edinburgh, and the New American Cyclopedia, the Conversations-Lexicon, Herzog's Real Encyclopädie für Prot. Theologie, and Ersch und Grüber's Cyclopädie, the latter still in course of publication, and of itself nearly filling one small case.

In the portion of the library devoted to the

Literature of Greece and Rome, the best editions have been selected, always in good and often in fine condition. There are choice Aldines and Elzevirs, with rare impressions from the offices of the Stephens, Foulis, Tonson, Baskerville, and other eminent printers, with several of the Wetstein, Barbou and Bipont editions.

There are of the classical writers and early Fathers *ten princeps* editions, Appian, Aristophanes, Plutarch's Morals, Plato, Diodorus Siculus, Philo Judæus, Eusebius, Photius, Theophylact, Athenagoras. The translation of Plato by Ficinus, 1473, and a Latin translation of Herodotus, folio, 1475, are believed to be the oldest books in the collection.

The *Archæological* section, and that of *Classical Topography*, *Mythology*, and, in a word, all that relates to the illustration of the ancient classics, in the researches and commentaries of modern scholars, embraces the great works of Montfauçon, the noble *Thesauri* of Græviius and Gronovius, Lipsius, Meursius, Winckelmann, Clinton; the architectural designs of Stewart and Revett, Canina's *Monuments of Ancient Rome*, Visconti's Iconographie, etc., the illustrated works of Hope and Gell; Vyse and Perring; Denon's and Jomard's illustrated works on the Pyramids; the plates of Dulong, Fontana, Bartoli; treatises on *Numismatics*, Latin, German and English; on

Architecture, from Vitruvius and Palladio to Chambers and Fergusson, and Stuart; on *Costume*, on *Typography;* on *Ancient*, and, to some extent, on *Modern Art*. In *Classical Topography*, there are Cramer, Leake, Mure, Rennell, Dennis, Nibby, Dodwell, Hobhouse, Wordsworth, Curtius, Wyse, Schliemann, etc.

In *Philology*, embracing a very wide range of signification, grammars and lexicons, upwards of seventy of each, in many languages; speculations on language and verbal criticism; histories of Literature and Bibliography, the library is "well mounted."

The prominent names in *Literary History* are Andres, Baillet, Fabricius, Gervinus, Guinguené, Hallam, Harles, Laharpe, Morhof, Müller, Mure, Gladstone, Schœll, Teuffel, Tiraboschi, Warton, Dunlop, Schlegel, Barante, Cave, Chambers, Duyckinck, Fauriel, Ticknor, Allibone, Menzel; while as subsidiary to this, the library is well supplied with bibliographical aid.

Ancient History, in the writings of the original historians, falls within the province of classical literature; but the library is also supplied with the best modern Histories of Greece and Rome, and approved versions of the standard authors in this department. Nor has *Modern History* been neglected, especially the Histories of our own country, and those of England, of France, and of Italy.

In *English History*, with its collateral illustrations, beside the ordinary standard authorities of Hume, S. Turner, Lingard, Hallam, Mackintosh, Macaulay, Mahon, etc., to and including Buckle, there are, in early—sometimes first—folio eds., the Saxon Chronicle, Bede, Matthew Paris, Usher, Buchanan, Bacon, Baker, Fuller, More, Herbert, Camden, Raleigh, Clarendon, Burnet, Whitlock, Daniel, Hackett, Oldmixon, Walker, and Rapin, with Houbraken's fine heads; a sprinkling of Memoirs of the Stuart and Georgian periods; a few rare old biographies of the seventeenth century, and some of later date: Ellis's *Letters*, Granger's *Biographical History*, Walpole's and other *Epistolary Collections*, Wordsworth's *Ecclesiastical Biography*, Harleian Miscellany.

American History, though by no means a speciality, includes original folio editions of Smith's *Virginia* and Cotton Mather's *Magnalia*, Dickenson's *Farmer's Letters*, Lee's *Memoirs*, lately brought into notice by the able monograph of Mr. Moore, Graham's *Letters on Vermont*, Journals of Madam Knight and Rev. Mr. Buckingham, Antiquitates Americanæ, and the rare original tract of Denton, of which a few years since but two copies were known to be in the country; some of the early French travellers, Rochefoucauld, Volney, Michaud, Chateaubriand; some half dozen of the older State Histories; the best lives of the great statesmen of the country; the political classics—collected writings of Washington, Adams, Jefferson, Hamilton, Webster, Franklin; the Federalist, original edition, 2 vols. 18mo; Documentary History of the State of New York; American Archives; State Papers; Diplomatic Correspondence; Journals of Congress; Annual Register.

With *Italian History*, the library is well provided, in a body of authors, including the works of Bentivoglio, Botta, Costanza, Denina, Giannone, Guicciardini, Machiavelli, Muratori, Nani, Pignotti, Palavicini, Sandini, Sismondi, Segni, Villani, Varchi.

In *French History*, the collection is not equally rich, yet there are Duchesne, Comines, Froissart, Monstrelet, Davila, De Thou, Sully, Voltaire, Rollin, Grimm, with the modern school of Sismondi, Guizot, Thiers, Thierry, Martin, Mignet, and Michelet; Historique Annuaire and Memoirs relating to the Revolution and to Napoleon.

A number of valuable works on *Geography* and *Chronology*—" the eyes of history "—are here, consisting of old Treatises, modern Tables and Charts, and a good collection of *Voyages* and *Travels*.

In *Continental Literature*, the German portion of

the library, exclusive of a few volumes of History, Political Science, Philology, and Classical Archæology, is chiefly confined to elegant literature; a choice collection of poetry, fiction, the drama, and æsthetical criticism.

Italian Literature is as well cared for as History, and includes several fine editions of standard authors, and a few uncommonly rare works. There is some Law and Theology; rare editions of the novelists, Boccaccio (1549 and 1761), Bandello, Sachetti; a set of Italian Economists in fifty volumes. In poetry, there are choice copies of Dante, 1578; Tasso, 1721 and 1761; Alfieri, (Pisa;) Bembo, 1st edition; Petrarch (1550, 1582;) Pulci, 1731.

Beside the historians, the scientific memoirs, and the elementary scientific treatises, there is little of *French Literature;* a few old novelists, as Scarron, Sarasin, and Rabelais, the great dramatists, fine quarto editions of Rousseau, Montesquieu, Fenelon, Pascal—choice, what there is, but little of it.

In *English Literature*, the library contains all the great old prose writers of the 16th, 17th and 18th centuries, who have written upon Theology, Morals and History, while the more substantial portion of the literature of the present has not been neglected.

Of *Prose Fiction*, the first demand of the Circulating, and the last of the College Library proper, unless the humorous sketches of Mr. Irving be included under that head, there is not—except the Waverley Novels, which are regarded as literary illustrations of history—strictly speaking, an English novel in the library.

In *Metaphysical* and *Moral Philosophy*, in *Logic*, in *Rhetoric*, in *Æsthetical Philosophy*, in *Treatises on Education*, the library possesses the sterling authors, Greek, Latin, French and English, from Aristotle and Plato to Cousin and Sir William Hamilton; while the great German writers, though not so fully represented, are not neglected.

The Law Library contains a complete series of the reports and statutes of the United States, and of the reports of the State of New York, with the most valuable of those of other States; a full series of the English reports from the Year-books to the present time, with several editions of the English statutes, and the principal treatises on American and English law. It embraces many editions of the body of the civil law, and the treatises of the most eminent commentators upon it, with many works of interest in Scotch, German, French, Italian, and other foreign law.

It includes the original law library of William Samuel Johnson, the first President of Columbia

College after the Revolution, and one of the framers of the Constitution of the United States, for which the college is indebted to the liberality of his descendant, the Hon. William Samuel Johnson, of Stratford, Connecticut. It has been further enriched by another donation of peculiar historic interest, from John Jay, Esq., of Bedford, New York, embracing the law library of his grandfather, John Jay, the first Chief-Justice of the United States.

The number of volumes in the library is about 4,000.

The library is open for the use of the students during the term from nine o'clock A. M. to ten o'clock P. M., when those who desire it pursue their studies, especially in the preparation of cases for the moot court. The central position of the school renders it easily accessible. It is quite near the Astor Library, to which students have access, and the law department of which contains several thousand volumes, including a very extensive series of English and American reports, with a valuable and rare collection of works on foreign law, and a full collection of French cases, ancient and modern.

The Library of the School of Mines was founded when the school was established—in the fall of 1864. At this time, when the connection subsisting between the school and the college proper was not quite so intimate as it now is, the income of the college was small, and it was felt that no appropriation of money could be made either to found the special library or to meet its current expenses. The short roll of students partaking of the benefits of the school during its first year or two were permitted to consult the books in the Academic Library; and their special needs were further recognized by devoting part of the annual library appropriation to the purchase of certain much-needed books. Subsequently, about one thousand volumes were transferred from this library and deposited for the use of the school in a room set aside for the purpose. This was the nucleus of the present library. To these were soon added many volumes of valuable works procured in exchange for about five hundred duplicate volumes of Reports of Natural History Surveys of the Several States and Territories, generously donated to the school by various authorities.

When the funds of the college grew more ample, an annual appropriation of $500 was made for the benefit of the library. This sum has been increased from time to time until, in 1870, it reached the sum of $2,000, which is the amount of the present annual appropriation.

The total amount of appropriations thus far made is about $17,000.

The library now contains about 7,000 volumes, half of which are volumes of periodical publications. The several departments which are embraced within the library are Chemistry, general, analytical and applied; Engineering, civil, mining and mechanical; Geology, Mineralogy, Botany, Zoology, Physics and Mechanics. It is particularly strong in the standard works pertaining to chemistry, analytical and applied; metallurgy, mineralogy and mining engineering. One of the most valuable features of the library is its extensive collection of periodical publications: complete series of Comptes Rendus; Poggendorff's Annalen; Philosophical Magazine; Erdman's Journal; Annales des Mines; Dingler's Journal; Annalen der Chemie u. Pharmacie; Annales de Chimie et Physique; Silliman's Journal, etc. Nearly eighty periodical publications are regularly received and kept on file in the library. These embrace the more important official reports of departments of government pertaining to the specialties of the school, and all the more valuable foreign and American private journals and reviews.

The systematic books embrace many rare and valuable individual works. Among these the Cavendish edition of Gmelin's Handworterbuch,

17 vols.; Palæontographica: Beiträge zur naturgeschichte der vorwelt, 25 vols.; Works of the Palæontographical Society, London, 25 vols.; and the chief editions, in English, French and German, of the principal works of Keil, Percy, Combes, Ponson, Gaetschman and Rittenger.

The library contains many volumes and portfolios of plates. Two of the most valuable and rare series of this description recently added (by donation) are the collection of plates to illustrate the light-house system of the United States, and "Collection des Dessins distribués aux éléves de l'Ecole Impériales des Ponts et Chaussées à Paris." Peculiarly interesting at this time is the full collection of the literature pertaining to the World's *Exhibitions held at London, Paris, Vienna, etc.*

The growth of the library has been very much augmented by generous donations from official sources and individuals interested in the school. Two hundred bound volumes and five hundred pamphlets have recently been added by bequest of the late H. F. Q. D'Aligney.

The Botanical Library contains twelve hundred and forty volumes. Besides embracing most of the books required for ordinary investigations, it is rich in scarce memoirs and separate papers received from their authors, such as cannot be purchased, and yet are often of greater value to the scientific investigator than costly volumes.

CABINETS AND COLLECTIONS.

In addition to such as have already been noted in the account of the School of Mines, there are, in the Academic Department:

A chemical and geological cabinet and collection illustrating fully elementary chemistry and geology, embracing the original New York State Cabinet of Geology, a collection of minerals and a valuable cabinet of rare chemicals; also a full set of chemical apparatus :

A set of models illustrating the subject of geometry of two and three dimensions; Schröder's Models of Descriptive Geometry, Standard Metre, etc.; a full set of surveying instruments, as chains, surveyor's compass, pocket compass, transit, level, plane table, theodolite, etc.:

A mechanical collection, embracing models of pulleys, levers, screw, inclined plane, parallelogram of forces, Atwood's machine, reversible pendulum, air pump, aerostatic apparatus, hydrostatic apparatus, balance and apparatus for specific gravity, etc., Schœdler's mechanical movements illustrating the subject of mechanics in all its branches :

Maps, globes, lantern and apparatus for illustrating the subject of astronomy ; a forty-six inch transit instrument by Troughton & Simms, an equatorially-mounted refractor of five-inch aperture, to which is attached a spectroscope with the dispersive power of thirteen flint glass prisms of fifty-five degrees, by Alvan Clarke; a set of comparison apparatus with electrodes, Plücker's tubes, coil, etc., accompanies the spectroscope ; altitude and azimuth instrument, declination transit, chronometer and break-circuit chronometer, heliostatic mirrors, sextant, etc., etc. :

A large and complete physical apparatus, among the pieces of which may be mentioned a Foucault's pendulum, 26 feet in length, and a complete Foucault gyroscope by Froment ; a fine cathetometer by Grünow, a spherometer, a comparateur, standard U. S. yard, standard metre, and a horizontal pendulum arranged for quantitative work:

Acoustic apparatus, such as (e. g.), Helmholtz's apparatus for the reproduction of the vowel sounds; Seebeck's syren ; a complete phonautograph ; a set of Meldes' tuning forks, Lüssajous' tuning forks and vibrating microscope ; apparatus for the refraction of sound ; a set of Helmholtz's resonators and vowel-forks :

Magnetic and electrical apparatus, of which may be mentioned a Lamont's declination compass, Wiedemann's galvanometer, Grünow's spark-micrometer, torsion balance, and sine and tangent compass; a Siemens' unit and an original Holtz machine; a large Richie coil; also Ruhmkorff coil and a diamagnetic apparatus:

An extensive optical apparatus, of which may be noted, Rutherfurd's automatic train of six prisms, ruled plates by the same for measuring wave lengths; apparatus for conical refraction, various sections of wave surfaces, Fessel's and Whedtstone's wave machines; Jamin's interferential refractor, Duboscq's apparatus for studying the interference and refraction of light, a large Nachet inverted microscope; polarizing apparatus for projection. Some of the pieces of this latter may be also mentioned on account of their size, such as a double refracting prism (3″) three inches in diameter, a Nicol's prism (2½″) two and one-half inches diam. and (7″) seven inches long.; a Foucault prism (4″) four inches in diameter, and (7″) seven inches in length; etc., etc.:

A botanical collection containing about sixty thousand species, phænograms and cryptograms: it is peculiarly rich in what are called *type specimens*, that is, the identical plants named by the authors who have described or noticed them in their published works: it possesses extensive collections of plants from the North Pacific Exploring Expedition, from Commodore Perry's Japan Expedition, from the various expeditions of Fremont, and from the explorations of North America, even within the Arctic Circle, besides many rare and valuable specimens from all parts of the world: it embraces the collection of the late Prof. John Torrey, which is valuable as containing the original specimens from which the "Flora of North America" was prepared; the Meissner-Crooke collection which is the authority of the polygonaceæ, proteaceæ, thymelæaceæ, etc., of De Candolles Prodromus; the "Chapman" collection containing the originals, from which was published the "Flora of the Southern United States," and also a small collection made by the late A. Halsey.

PRIZES, SCHOLARSHIPS AND FELLOWSHIPS.

In the Academic Department, the following scheme of prizes, etc., obtains:

I.—For Proficiency in German.—After the concluding examination there shall be awarded to the best student in German, in the Junior class, a prize of money, or its equivalent, at his option, of *thirty dollars*; and to the next best, a prize of *twenty dollars*.

In like manner, to the best student in the Sophomore class, a prize, as before, of *thirty dollars ;* and to the next best, one of *twenty dollars.*

II.—PRIZE OF THE ALUMNI ASSOCIATION.—A prize of *fifty dollars* in money, or its equivalent, at the option of the receiver, established by the Association of the Alumni of Columbia College, was first awarded at the commencement in June, 1858.

It is to be given " to the most faithful and deserving student of the graduating class."

Three names are selected by the Faculty, and submitted to the class, who, from these three, designate one to receive the prize.

III.—SCHEME OF TWO ANNUAL SEMINARY PRIZES. *Founded November,* 1851, *in Columbia College, by the Rev. Dr. John McVickar, for the Society for Promoting Religion and Learning, and for which an endowment of* $1,000 *is provided on the following conditions :*

1. The first to be entitled " The Society's Greek Seminary Prize of Thirty Dollars," to be annually competed for among such members of the graduating class as shall have given in their names to the President at least one month previous to such competition, as candidates for the General Theological Seminary of the Protestant Episcopal

Church, each student giving in his name as "competitor" to designate the prize for which he contends, and to be confined to the choice then made. The examination for such prize to be held publicly in the chapel, and separate from the general examination. To be on:

I. The Epistles of the New Testament (in Greek) "ad aperturam libri."

II. On some one of the early Greek Fathers, to be designated at the time of noticing the prize; or, if none be designated, then upon some portion of *Chrysostom* or *Athanasius*, at the choice of the student.

The decision to be with the President and the Greek Professor.

2. The second, to be entitled "The Society's English Seminary Prize of Twenty Dollars," to be annually competed for as before, and to consist in the production of an essay (to be publicly read, or not, as the President may determine,) of the ordinary length of a pulpit discourse, on some subject connected with the course of evidences on which the class has been engaged; such subject to be selected by the Professor of the evidences, and given out by him at the time of notice; and the prize to be adjudged, as before, by the President

and Professor of that branch, such decision to have respect to—

I. The general ability and soundness of the essay;

II. Its logical and demonstrative form; and

III. The pure Saxon style and idiom in which it is written.

The name of the successful candidate to be enrolled in a suitable book to be provided for that purpose, lettered appropriately and kept on the library table; to be announced with other honors on the commencement day; and also recorded honorably in the Society's books.

IV.—JUNIOR PRIZES IN GREEK.—*For the encouragement of proficiency in the Greek language and literature, two prizes have been established, to be annually awarded to members of the Junior class under the following conditions:*

An annual prize of the value of three hundred dollars shall be awarded to the student of the Junior class who shall pass the best examination on an entire play of Æschylus, Sophocles, or Euripides, which has not been a subject of college study in that class; and a second prize of one hundred and fifty dollars shall be awarded to the student of the Junior class whose examination shall appear to be next in order of merit, both under the following conditions:

The prizes shall be open for competition to such students of the Junior class as shall have been members of the college for two years, and shall not have appeared in any term or examination record deficient in scholarship in any department of study.

The examination for the prizes shall be held within one week after the concluding college examination, and shall be conducted by a committee of three appointed by the President, who are to be selected from among the Alumni not connected with the college, and the Professors in the classical departments. It shall be in writing, and shall have reference to the subject-matter as well as form of the play, the title of which shall have been assigned at the beginning of the academic year by the Professor of Greek with the approval of the President.

The examiners may in their discretion subject all or any of the competitors to a *viva voce* examination in addition to the written examination above described.

The competitors shall all be subject to the same tests.

The result of the examination shall be estimated

according to a scale of values previously assigned to the questions.

The student whose performances shall receive under this regulation the highest number of marks shall be entitled to the first prize, provided such number does not fall below a fixed minimum standard previously determined, and the student whose total is next in amount to the highest shall be entitled to the second prize, with the same proviso.

The names of the successful competitors shall appear in the college catalogue, and the President shall cause the same to be published in three daily papers of this city as soon as the award is made known.

V.—SENIOR PRIZES IN ENGLISH.—On the 2d of June, 1873, the following resolution was adopted by the Board of Trustees:

Resolved, That two prizes in Rhetoric and English Composition of $100 and $50 be established, to be competed for by written theses at the end of the Senior year; and that it be referred to the Board of the College to report suitable regulations.

The following are the rules and regulations established by the Faculty:

1. The subject shall be prescribed every year except the first (1873-74), on or before the first day of November.

2. The Essays shall be delivered to the Professor of English on or before the first day of May.

3. The Essays shall be copied in a hand different from the author's.

4. They shall bear a motto or a fictitious name, and be accompanied by a sealed note repeating the motto or name, disclosing the author and containing a declaration on honor that the accompanying essay is the authentic genuine production of the author, in form as follows, viz.:—

> I hereby declare, on my honor, that the essay bearing the motto " ——" was written by me, without undue aid from persons or books, and is, in the usual sense of authorship, the authentic, genuine production of A, B, or C.

5. The essays shall be submitted to a committee of three, whose decision shall be final, and the appended notes shall be opened at commencement.

6. If in the opinion of the Committee of Judges for the year none of the essays is worthy of the first prize, the second shall be awarded, and if none be worthy of first or second prize, both may be withheld for that year.

7. No student deficient in the studies of the year in any one department shall be admitted to the competition.

VI.—Prize Scholarships and Fellowships.—By resolutions of the Board of Trustees, there have been established in the College fourteen Scholarships, of the annual value of one hundred dollars each; and two Fellowships, of the annual value of five hundred dollars each.

Four of the Scholarships are offered for competition to members of the Freshman class, one in Latin, one in Greek, one in Mathematics, and one in Rhetoric.

Four are offered for competition to members of the Sophomore class, one in Latin, one in Greek, one in Mathematics, and one in History.

Six are offered for competition to members of the Junior class, three in literary and three in scientific studies, viz.: one in Latin, one in Greek, one in Logic and English Literature, one in Chemistry, one in Mechanics, and one in Physics.

The examinations for these Scholarships are to be held immediately after the final examination of the classes for the year.

The Fellowships are offered for competition to members of the Senior class at the close of the academic course. One of these is a Fellowship in Literature, the other a Fellowship in Science. The subjects of examination for the Fellowship in Literature are Greek, Latin, and Intellectual and Moral Philosophy; and those for the Fellowship in Science are Chemistry, Geology, Astronomy, the Calculus, and Physics.

The Fellows are required to continue their studies, under the direction of the President, for the term of three years; at the end of which time the Fellowship expires by limitation. They may study at the college, or elsewhere, in the United States or abroad; but in any case they will report to the President at such intervals and in such mode as he may prescribe.

In the School of Law a series of prizes has been established, to be awarded to such members of the school as shall have attained the highest excellence in their respective classes. Three such prizes are given in the Department of Municipal Law. They were first awarded in the spring of 1860, and will hereafter be continued yearly. Competitors for these prizes must have pursued the full course of study prescribed by the rules.

In the Department of Municipal Law the sums awarded will be:

For the first prize, two hundred and fifty dollars.
For the second prize, one hundred and fifty dollars.
For the third prize, one hundred dollars.

The rules respecting the adjudication of prizes are as follows:

1. There shall be an examination of the candidates for prizes at the close of each collegiate year.

Candidates must have been connected with the Law School for two collegiate years.

2. The tests of excellence shall be twofold:

a. By an examination in writing, in answer to printed questions.

b. By essays prepared upon such legal topics as may be suggested.

The prizes shall be adjudicated upon the combined excellence of the essays and of the examinations. Diligence and regularity of attendance upon the prescribed exercises of the school shall also form an element in reaching the conclusion.

3. The following directions must be observed by the candidates in preparing essays:

a. The essays shall be written on white letter paper of the best quality, with a margin of an inch wide. Only two pages of each sheet shall be written upon. The chirography must be plain and legible. The essays shall not exceed ten sheets in length, or three-fourths of an hour in delivery, if spoken.

b. The positions taken in the essays shall, if debatable, be fortified by the citation of authorities. Where the point is reasonably well settled, a single decisive and leading authority will suffice. In other cases more are admissible.

c. Conciseness and clearness of expression, accuracy of statement, and close reasoning, should be carefully studied by the essayists.

d. Each essay must be signed with a fictitious name and be accompanied by a sealed envelope, upon the outside of which shall be written the fictitious name attached to the essay, and within, a slip of paper containing the real name of the author. The essays shall be delivered to the Professor of Municipal Law on or before April 28th. The essays shall belong to the College.

4. The examination upon the printed questions shall be made as follows:

a. Those who intend to compete for the prizes shall enter their names in a book provided for that purpose, upon the day of examination. If among these persons there are any who have been wanting in a reasonable degree of punctuality, they shall be informed before examination that they may fail to obtain the prize.

b. The Professor of Municipal Law shall call a session of the candidates at such a time, near the close of the collegiate year, as may be convenient. He shall furnish at the opening of the session the printed papers to the students, who shall write their answers in his presence upon paper similar to that provided for the essays, with similar margin. During this session there shall be a general silence observed, except in regard to such necessary questions as may be addressed to the Professor, and there shall be especially no communication of the candidates with each other respecting answers. A failure to observe these rules will work a forfeiture of the right to receive a prize.

c. After the session is finished, each set of answers to the printed questions shall be signed by the candidate with the fictitious name attached to his essay, and handed in to the Professor presiding. The answers shall belong to the College.

5. The essays and answers shall thereupon be transmitted to a Committee on Prizes, consisting of three members of the legal profession, who are to be selected by the Law Committee of the College. The report of this committee will be communicated to the Professor of Municipal Law in writing.

6. The names of the successful candidates will be announced at the Law Commencement.

7. The prizes shall be awarded, at the option of the recipient, in money, medals, or books. Where no notice is given to the contrary, the award will be in money, until otherwise ordered.

In the School of Mines there are two annual prizes of fifty dollars each—one to the student of the first year who passes the best written and experimental examination in Qualitative Analysis, and one to the student of the school who gives evidence of the most thorough knowledge of the theory and practice of Assaying. These prizes are called Torrey Prizes, in honor of the late Prof. John Torrey.

In the School of Medicine the scheme of prizes is as follows:

I. FACULTY PRIZES.—Two prizes are awarded annually by the Faculty for the best two graduating Theses presented during the year, viz.: A *First Prize* of Fifty Dollars, and a *Second Prize* of Twenty-five Dollars. Competing Theses should be submitted to the Secretary of the Faculty,—in the case of Fall candidates, by September 1; in the case of Winter candidates, by February 1.

II. ALUMNI ASSOCIATION PRIZE.—This is an annual Prize of not less than Two Hundred Dollars, open for competition to all Alumni of the School. It is awarded for the best *Medical Essay* submitted, if deemed sufficiently meritorious, upon any subject the writer may select. The Prize Committee is appointed annually by the Association at their Annual Meeting on the evening before the Commencement. Competing Essays must be marked by a device or motto, and accompanied by an envelope similarly marked, containing the name and address of the author. They must be submitted to the Prize Committee on or before the 15th day of February in each year.

No award was made in 1875. The Prize for 1876 will be Four Hundred Dollars.

III.—STEVENS TRIENNIAL PRIZE.—Established by the late ALEXANDER H. STEVENS, M. D., former President of the School, on the following plan:

Each Prize, to be awarded triennially, is to consist of the interest yielded by the principal fund during the preceding three years, and will amount to Two Hundred Dollars.

The administration of the Prize is entrusted to a commission, consisting of the President of the College of Physicians and Surgeons (School of Medicine), the President of the Alumni Association, and the Professor of Physiology, in the same institution.

The following are the subjects for the Triennial Prize of 1876:

1st. The History of Epidemic Diseases in the United States, from 1860 to 1870; statements as to locality, dates, extent of prevalence, and mortality, to be authenticated by appropriate references. The question of treatment is not to form a part of the above subject.

2d. The use of the Spectroscope in its application to scientific and practical medicine.

The competing essays on either of the above subjects must be sent in to the President of the School, on or before the first day of January, 1876. Each essay must be designated by a device or motto, and must be accompanied by a sealed envelope, bearing the same device or motto, and containing the name and address of the author. The envelope belonging to the successful essay will be opened, and the name of the author announced, at the Annual Commencement, in March, 1876; at which time the subjects for the next triennial prize (1879) will also be announced.

The prize is open for universal competition.

IV. JOSEPH MATHER SMITH PRIZE.—The fund for this Prize is endowed by the relatives of the late Dr. SMITH, as a memorial of his services as Professor from 1826 to 1866. Under its provisions an Annual Prize of One Hundred Dollars will be awarded for the best essay on the subject for the year, presented by an alumnus of this School, or member of the graduating class. The Prize Committee, consisting of the President of the School, the Professor of Pathology and Practical Medicine, and the President of the Alumni Association, shall designate each year the subject for the following year. The competing essays should be sent to the President of the School on or before the 1st of January in each year; each essay to be signed with a device or motto, and accompanied by a sealed envelope inscribed with the same device or motto, and containing the name of the author. The envelope of the successful Essay to be opened, and the Prize awarded at the Annual Commencement.

The subject of the Prize to be awarded in March, 1877, is *Hygiene, in either of its Special Departments.*

V. Otis Prize.—This is an Annual Prize of Fifty Dollars, established by Professor Otis, for the best Report of the Clinical and Didactic Lectures on Venereal Diseases, given in the School during the previous year.

VI. Thomas Prize.—This is an Annual Prize of a case of Obstetrical and Gynæcological Instruments, established by Professor Thomas, for the best written Report of the Cases presented at his Clinic during the Winter Session.

VII. Seguin Prize.—This is an Annual Prize of a Microscope, established by Professor Seguin, for the most deserving Report of the Cases presented at his Clinic during the Winter Session.

VIII. Vanderpoel Prize.—This is a Special Prize for the year 1875–6, offered by Dr. S. O. Vanderpoel, for the best Examination in Anatomy. It consists of the sum of Fifty Dollars.

Financial Statement.

The following statement, taken from the last annual statement made to the Board of Regents of the University of the State of New York, sets forth the financial position of the college:

1. Description and value of college buildings, etc.

The buildings of the college consist of the main building devoted to instruction in the academic department; the chapel and library; the west wing now used for the Herbarium, a faculty room, students' study and waiting-room, and the residence of the janitor; the School of Mines buildings, for the collections and instruction of that school; and a house for the President. These occupy the grounds comprising the block of ground bounded by Fourth and Madison Avenues, Forty-ninth and Fiftieth Streets.

Value of college buildings and grounds appurtenant thereto, including buildings recently erected for the School of Mines . .	$530,000
The number of volumes in the general library, including bound pamphlets, is 17,339. Its total estimated value is	46,000

In the law library, in use for the Law School, there are about 4,030 volumes, of the estimated value of	$8,500
The library of the School of Mines consists of 5,963 volumes, of the estimated value of	22,000
In the botanical library there are 1,220 volumes, of the estimated value of . .	4,100
The chemical, philosophical, astronomical and mathematical apparatus and cabinets, exclusive of those of the School of Mines, and exclusive of the Herbarium, are valued at	29,500
The chemical and philosophical apparatus and cabinets of the School of Mines are valued at	122,000
The Herbarium is valued at	25,000
Total amount invested as above for purposes of instruction	$787,700

---

2. Description and Value of other College Property.

Real estate. The college owns land in the city of New York in College Place, Park Place, Murray, Barclay, and Greenwich Streets, subject to long leases of divers and separate lots. It is estimated that this land will yield in the next year a net revenue of five per cent. upon a capital of	2,128,260.00

The college also holds two hundred and sixty-four lots of land (as now divided) situated between the Fifth and Sixth Avenues and Forty-seventh and Fifty-first Streets. All these lots are under lease, and improved by the erection of buildings which in all cases belong to the lessees. It is difficult to ascertain the assessed value of the interest of the college therein, except so far as it may be estimated from the rents. The rents reserved by the leases of this estate now yield a net income upon a capital of $2,041,786.80

PERSONAL PROPERTY.—The college held at the end of the financial year, on the 30th September, 1875:

Invested by deposit with New York Life and Trust Co. .	$20,951.12	
Cash balance at end of year .	1,668.12	
Invested on Mortgage . .	366,653.21	
Advances to dean of School of Mines	1,000.00	
		390,272.45
Showing the total estimated value of the property which can be applied to the general purposes of the college to be . .		$4,560,319.25
The Gebhard fund is applicable only to the support of a professorship of the German language and literature, and is now invested on bond and mortgage. Its amount is		21,375.00
Total estimated value of the property of the college other than such as is included under head one		$4,581,694.25

---

3. DEBTS.

The total amount of debt contracted by the Trustees, and remaining unpaid at the end of the year was $41,240.00

No debt was contracted during the year. The interest accrued on the debt was . . 4,038.24

4. REVENUE.

Amount charged for tuition fees of academic students . .	$12,100.00	
Of law students	47,283.18	
Of students of School of Mines .	27,275.00	
For diplomas in the college .	230.00	
For diplomas in Law School .	1,050.00	
		$87,938.18
Receipts from students of School of Mines for breakage and supplies		$6,186.93
Proceeds of old material in college cellars .		118.50
Interest derived from the personal funds of the college other than the Gebhard fund was		1,764.94
Rents for the year collected		204,094.34
Interest on rents		186.75
Rents in arrear and unpaid		798.00
Total revenue from above sources . .		$301,087.64

---

5. EXPENDITURE.—The whole expenditures applicable to said income, paid or payable for said year are as follows:

Salaries of officers of the college, ...	$72,734.22
Interest accrued during the year on debts of the college	4,038.24
Ordinary repairs of college property . .	918.86
Fuel and all other incidental expenses of the college	17,302.51
Salaries of officers of the Law School . .	9,975.00
Repairs of the Law School	2,006.65

Fuel and all other incidental expenses of such school	$27,622.08
Salaries of officers of School of Mines . .	34,325.63
Repairs of such school	413.00
Fuel and all other incidental expenses of such school	37,722.41
Expenses of Treasurer's and Clerk's offices, and of estate, including taxes . . .	1,048.35
Total	$208,106.95

SENATUS ACADEMICUS,

1876

TRUSTEES OF COLUMBIA COLLEGE.

NAMES.	RESIDENCES.
HAMILTON FISH, LL. D., Chairman of the Board.	251 East 17th Street.
SAMUEL B. RUGGLES, LL. D	24 Union Square.
WILLIAM BETTS, LL. D	122 East 30th Street.
BENJAMIN I. HAIGHT, S. T. D., LL. D.	56 West 26th Street.
ROBERT RAY	363 West 28th Street.
GOUVERNEUR M. OGDEN, Treasurer.	187 Fulton, h. 89 W. 10th Street.
EDWARD L. BEADLE, M. D	Poughkeepsie.
MANCIUS S. HUTTON, S. T. D.	47 East Ninth Street.
HORATIO POTTER, S.T.D., LL. D., D. C. L	38 East 22d Street.
LEWIS M. RUTHERFURD	175 Second Avenue.
JOHN C. JAY, M. D	24 West 48th Street.
WILLIAM C. SCHERMERHORN	49 West 23d Street.
MORGAN DIX, S. T. D.	27 West 25th Street.
FREDERICK A. P. BARNARD, S. T. D., LL. D., L. H. D.	College Green.
SAMUEL BLATCHFORD, LL.D	12 West 22d Street.
STEPHEN P. NASH	11 West 19th Street.
CHARLES R. SWORDS	156 Broadway,
ANTHONY HALSEY, Clerk.	291 Broadway.
JOSEPH W. HARPER	331 Pearl Street.
CORNELIUS R. AGNEW, M. D	244 Madison Avenue.
EVERT A. DUYCKINCK	20 Clinton Place.
JAMES W. BEEKMAN	5 East 34th Street.
AARON E. VANDERPOEL	114 East 16th Street.
CHARLES A. SILLIMAN	Troy, N. Y.

TRUSTEES.—SCHOOL OF MEDICINE.

NAMES.	RESIDENCES.
EDWARD G. LUDLOW, M. D	School of Medicine.
JOHN P. CROSBY	150 Lexington Avenue.
GURDON BUCK, M. D	46 West 29th Street.
DANIEL D. LORD	45 West 19th Street.
JAMES W. BEEKMAN	5 East 34th Street.
BENJAMIN R. WINTHROP	20 Union Square.
EDWARD L. BEADLE, M. D	Poughkeepsie, N. Y.
FREDERICK A. CONKLING	27 East 10th Street.
SULLIVAN H. WESTON, D. D	3 East 45th Street.
WILLIAM BETTS, LL. D	122 East 30th Street.
CAMBRIDGE LIVINGSTON	44 West 22d Street.
JARED LINSLY, M. D	22 Lafayette Place.
JOHN J. CRANE, M. D	31 West 21st Street.
ELLSWORTH ELIOT, M. D	48 West 36th Street.
JAMES L. BANKS, M. D	47 Fifth Avenue.
ROBERT G. REMSEN	87 Fifth Avenue.
EDWARD DELAFIELD	46 East 22d Street.
WILLARD PARKER, M. D	41 East 12th Street.
JOHN G. ADAMS, M. D	
JOHN SHERWOOD	423 West 41st Street.
FREDERICK A. P. BARNARD, S. T. D., LL. D., L. H. D	Columbia College.
SAMUEL T. HUBBARD, M. D	27 West 9th Street.
ALFRED S. PURDY, M. D Pres. Alumni Association.	30 West 33d Street.
ALONZO CLARK, M. D., *ex-officio*	23 East 21st Street.
THOMAS F. COCK, M. D	233 Madison Avenue.

ACADEMIC DEPARTMENT.

FACULTY.

FREDERICK A. P. BARNARD, S. T. D., LL. D., L. H. D........................College Green.
President.

HENRY DRISLER, LL. D.................. 48 West 46th Street.
Jay Professor of the Greek Language and Literature.

NAMES.	RESIDENCES.

HENRY I. SCHMIDT, S. T. D. .... 126 West 43d Street.
Gebhard Professor of the German Language and Literature.

CHARLES A. JOY, PH. D. .... 117 East 70th Street.
Professor of Chemistry.

CHARLES DAVIES, LL. D. .... Fishkill Landing.
Emeritus Professor of the Higher Mathematics.

WILLIAM G. PECK, LL. D. .... Columbia College.
Professor of Mathematics and Astronomy.

CHARLES MURRAY NAIRNE, L. H. D. ... 163 West 34th Street.
Professor of Moral and Intellectual Philosophy and English Literature.

J. HOWARD VAN AMRINGE, A. M. .... 165 West 46th Street.
Professor of Mathematics and Secretary of the Faculty.

OGDEN N. ROOD, A. M. .... 341 East 15th Street.
Professor of Mechanics and Physics.

CHARLES SHORT, LL. D. .... 24 West 60th Street.
Professor of the Latin Language and Literature.

JOHN W. BURGESS, A. M. .... Columbia College.
Professor of History, Political Science and International Law.

OTHER OFFICERS.

AUGUSTUS C. MERRIAM, A. M. .... Columbia College.
Tutor in Greek and Latin.

JOHN D. QUACKENBOS, A. M., M. D. ... 331 West 28th Street.
Tutor in Rhetoric and History.

EDWARD J. HALLOCK, A. M. .... 115 East 56th Street.
Assistant in General Chemistry.

MAGNUS C. IHLSENG, C. E., E. M. .... Columbia College.
Assistant in Physics.

WILLIAM H. INGERSOLL, A. M., E. M., LL. B. .... Columbia College.
Assistant in the Astronomical Observatory.

CORNELIUS R. DUFFIE, S. T. D. .... 233 Lexington Avenue.
Chaplain.

NAMES.	RESIDENCES.
BEVERLEY R. BETTS, A. M.	122 East 30th Street.

Librarian.

STEPHEN R. WEEKS.....................Columbia College.

Assistant Librarian.

SCHOOL OF LAW.

FACULTY.

FREDERICK A. P. BARNARD, S. T. D., LL. D..Columbia College.

President.

THEODORE W. DWIGHT, LL. D........ 8 Great Jones Street.

Warden of the Law School and Professor of Municipal Law.

CHARLES MURRAY NAIRNE, L. H. D...163 West 34th St.

Professor of Ethics of Jurisprudence.

JOHN ORDRONAUX, M. D., LL. D........Roslyn, L. I.

Professor of Medical Jurisprudence.

GEORGE CHASE, LL. B.................. 8 Great Jones Street.

Assistant Professor of Municipal Law.

JOHN W. BURGESS, A. M................Columbia College.

Professor of History, Political Science and International Law.

LECTURER.

GEORGE H. YEAMAN.....................294 Broadway.

SCHOOL OF MINES.

FACULTY.

FREDERICK A. P. BARNARD, S T. D., LL. D., L. H. D......................Columbia College.

President.

THOMAS EGLESTON, E. M., PH. D., LL. D. .... 10 Fifth Avenue.

Professor of Mineralogy and Metallurgy.

FRANCIS L. VINTON, E. M., C. E.......St. Denis Hotel.

Professor of Civil and Mining Engineering.

NAMES.	RESIDENCES.
CHARLES F. CHANDLER, PH. D., M. D., LL. D.	51 East 54th Street.
Professor of Analytical and Applied Chemistry. Dean of the Faculty.	
CHARLES A. JOY, PH. D.	117 East 70th Street.
Professor of General Chemistry.	
WILLIAM G. PECK, LL. D.	Columbia College.
Professor of Mechanics.	
J. HOWARD VAN AMRINGE, A. M.	165 West 46th Street.
Professor of Mathematics.	
OGDEN N. ROOD, A. M.	341 East 15th Street.
Professor of Physics.	
JOHN S. NEWBERRY, M. D., LL. D.	Columbia College.
Professor of Geology and Palæontology.	

INSTRUCTORS.

FREDERICK STENGEL, A. M. (in German)	122 Waverley Place.
JULES E. LOISEAU, A. B., LL. D. (in French)	23 East 33d Street.

ASSISTANTS.

ALEXIS A. JULIEN, A. M	Columbia College.
Assistant in Analytical Chemistry.	
ELWYN WALLER, A. M., E. M., PH. D.	33 West 15th Street.
Assistant in Analytical Chemistry.	
FREDERICK A. CAIRNS, A. M.	40 Grove Street.
Assistant in Analytical Chemistry.	
WILLIAM PISTOR, E. M.	413 West 21st Street.
Assistant in Drawing.	
I. W. RUSSELL	
Assistant in Geology.	
PIERRE DE PEYSTER RICKETTS, E. M.	50 West 50th Street.
Assistant in Assaying.	

NAMES.	RESIDENCES.
HENRY CARRINGTON BOLTON, A. M., PH. D.	49 West 51st Street.
Assistant in Analytical Chemistry.	
CHARLES ADAMS COLTON, E. M.	748 Fifth Street.
Assistant in Mineralogy.	
EDWARD JOHN HALLOCK, A. M.	115 East 56th Street.
Assistant in General Chemistry.	
JOHN KROM REES, A. M., E. M.	303 East 17th Street.
Assistant in Mathematics.	
WILLIAM HALSEY INGERSOLL, A. M., LL. B., E. M.	105 East 21st Street.
Assistant in the Astronomical Observatory.	
GRACIE S. ROBERTS, E. M.	88 Union Av. Brooklyn.
Assistant in Civil and Mining Engineering.	
JOHN HENRY CASWELL, A. B.	370 Fifth Avenue.
Assistant in Mineralogy.	
JAMES S. C. WELLS, PH. B.	Hackensack, N. J.
Assistant in Analytical Chemistry.	
MALVERN W. ILES, PH. B.	Columbia College.
Assistant in Analytical Chemistry.	
JOHN F. MEYER	Columbia College.
Registrar and Librarian.	

SCHOOL OF MEDICINE.

FACULTY.

ALONZO CLARK, M. D.	23 East 21st Street.
President and Professor of Pathology and Practical Medicine.	
WILLARD PARKER, M. D.	41 East 12th Street.
Professor of Clinical Surgery.	
JOHN C. DALTON, M. D.	41 West 48th Street.
Professor of Physiology and Hygiene.	
SAMUEL ST. JOHN, M. D.	208 West 43d Street.
Professor of Chemistry and Medical Jurisprudence.	

NAMES.	RESIDENCES.
THOMAS M. MARKOE, M. D.	20 West 30th Street.
Professor of Surgery.	
T. GAILLAIRD THOMAS, M. D.	294 Fifth Avenue.
Professor of Obstetrics and the Diseases of Women and Children.	
JOHN T. METCALFE, M. D.	18 West 30th Street.
Emeritus Professor of Clinical Medicine.	
HENRY B. SANDS, M. D.	35 West 33d Street.
Professor of Anatomy.	
JAMES W. McLANE, M. D.	46 West 23d Street.
Adjunct Professor of Obstetrics and the Diseases of Women and Children.	
THOMAS T. SABINE, M. D.	46 West 23d Street.
Adjunct Professor of Anatomy.	
CHARLES F. CHANDLER, Ph. D.	51 East 54th Street.
Adjunct Professor of Chemistry and Medical Jurisprudence.	
EDWARD CURTIS, M. D.	27 Washington Place.
Professor of Materia Medica and Therapeutics.	
FRANCIS DELAFIELD, M. D.	12 West 23d Street.
Adjunct Lecturer on Pathology and Practical Medicine.	
JOHN G. CURTIS, M. D.	101 West 40th Street.
Adjunct Lecturer on Physiology and Hygiene.	
WILLIAM DETMOLD, M. D.	38 East 9th Street.
Emeritus Professor of Clinical and Military Surgery.	
WILLIAM H. DRAPER, M. D.	4 East 37th Street.
Clinical Professor of Diseases of the Skin.	
CORNELIUS R. AGNEW, M. D.	244 Madison Avenue.
Clinical Professor of Diseases of the Eye and Ear.	
ABRAHAM JACOBI, M. D.	110 West 34th Street.
Clinical Professor of Diseases of Children.	
FESSENDEN N. OTIS, M. D.	108 West 34th Street.
Clinical Professor of Venereal Diseases.	
EDWARD C. SEGUIN, M. D.	41 West 20th Street.
Clinical Professor of Diseases of the Mind and Nervous System.	
GEORGE M. LEFFERTS, M. D.	333 West 22d Street.
Clinical Lecturer on Laryngoscopy and Diseases of the Throat.	

NAMES.	RESIDENCES.
CHARLES McBURNEY, M. D.	46 East 30th Street.
Demonstrator of Anatomy.	
CHARLES KELSEY, M. D.	48 East 30th Street
Assistant Demonstrator of Anatomy.	

FACULTY OF THE SPRING SESSION.

JAMES L. LITTLE, M. D.	266 West 42d Street.
Lecturer on Operative Surgery and Surgical Dressings.	
GEORGE G. WHEELOCK, M. D.	11 West 37th Street.
Lecturer on Physical Diagnosis.	
A. BRAYTON BALL, M. D.	38 West 36th Street.
Lecturer on Diseases of the Kidneys.	
ROBERT F. WEIR, M. D.	19 East 32d Street.
Lecturer on Diseases of the Genito-Urinary Organs.	
FRANK E. BECKWITH, M. D.	567 Lexington Avenue
Lecturer on Diseases of Children.	
MATTHEW D. MANN, M. D.	8 West 45th Street.
Lecturer on the Microscope as an Aid to Diagnosis.	

CLINICAL ASSISTANTS.

JAMES L. LITTLE, M. D.
JOHN T. KENNEDY, M. D.
HENRY F. WALKER, M. D.
CHARLES S. WARD, M. D.
ROBERT W. TAYLOR, M. D.
W. DE FOREST DAY, M. D.
WOOLSEY JOHNSON, M. D.
OREN D. POMEROY, M. D.
A. BRAYTON BALL, M. D.
ALBERT H. BUCK, M. D.
LUCIUS D. BULKLEY, M. D.
THOS. E. SATTERTHWAITE, M. D.
THOMAS A. McBRIDE, M. D.
FRANK P. KINNICUTT, M. D.
ISAAC ADLER, M. D.
SAMUEL B. ST. JOHN, M. D.
ROBERT F. WEIR, M. D.
DAVID WEBSTER, M. D.
W. H. VERMILYE, M. D.
GEORGE G. WHEELOCK, M. D.

GEORGE B. FOWLER, M. D.,
Curator of the College Museum.

AN APPENDIX

CONTAINING THE

ORIGINAL CHARTER

OF

COLUMBIA COLLEGE,

IN THE

CITY OF NEW YORK,

OCTOBER 31st, 1754;

WITH

THE ACTS OF THE LEGISLATURE

ALTERING AND AMENDING THE SAME,

OR RELATING TO THE COLLEGE.

THE

ORIGINAL CHARTER

OF

COLUMBIA COLLEGE.

GEORGE THE SECOND, by the grace of God, of Great Britain, France, and Ireland, King, Defender of the Faith, &c. *To all to whom* these presents shall come, *Greeting: Whereas*, by several acts of the Governour, Council, and General assembly of our Province of New York, divers sums of money have been Raised by Publick Lotteries, and appropriated for the founding, erecting, and establishing a College in our said Government, for the Education and Instruction of Youth in the Liberal Arts and Sciences: *And Whereas*, the Rector and inhabitants of the City of New York, in Communion of the Church of England, as by Law Established, for the encouraging and promoting the same good design, have sett apart a parcel of ground for that purpose, of upwards of Three Thousand Pounds value, belonging to the said Corporation, on the west side of the broadway, in the west ward of our City of New York, fronting easterly to Church street, between Barclay street and Murray street, four hundred and forty foot; And from thence running westerly, between and along the said Barclay street and Murray street, to the North River; *And also*, a street, from the middle of the said Land, Easterly to the Broadway, of ninety Foot, to be called Robinson street, And have declared that they are ready and desirous to Convey the said Land in Fee, to and for the use of a College, intended and proposed to be Erected and Established in our said Province, upon the terms in their said declaration mentioned: *And Whereas* our Loving Subjects, the Trustees, appointed in and by an act of the Governor, Council, and General Assembly of our said Province of New York, Intitled an Act for Vesting in Trustees the sum of three Thousand four Hundred and forty three Pounds eighteen shillings, by way of Lottery, for erecting a College within this Colony, esteeming the said Lands offered and sett apart by the said Rector and Inhabitants of the City of New York, in Communion of the Church of England, as by Law Established, the most convenient place for the Building, Erecting, and Establishing, a College, in our said Province, have, by their humble petition, presented to our trusty and well beloved *James De Lancey, Esq.*, our Lieutenant Governor and Commander in Chief of our said Province of New York, *In Council,* prayed our Letters patent of Incorporation for the Better Establishing, Erecting, and Building a College, on the said Lands, and the more Effectually Governing, Carrying on, and Promoting the same, and Instructing of Youth in the Liberal Arts and Sciences; *Wherefore, Wee,* being willing to Grant the Reasonable request and desire of our said Loving Subjects, and to Encourage the said good design of promoting a Liberal Education among them, and to make the same as Beneficial as may be, not only to the Inhabitants of our said Province of New York, But to all our Colonies and Territories in America, *Know Ye,* that Wee, considering the premisses, do, of our especial Grace, Certain Knowledge, and meer motion, by these presents, will Grant, Constitute, and ordain, that when, and as soon as the said Rector and Inhabitants of the City of New York, in Communion of the Church of England, as by Law established, shall legally convey and assure the said herein before mentioned Lands to the Corporation, or body politick, Erected and made by these our Letters patent, That there be erected and made on the said Lands, a College, and other Buildings and Improvements, for the use and conveniency of the same, which shall be called and Known by the name of *King's College*, for the Instruction and Education of Youth in the Learned Languages, and Liberal Arts and Sciences; *And* that in consideration of such Grant, to be made by the Rector and Inhabitants of the City of New York, in Communion of the Church of England, as by Law Established, the President of the said College, for the time being, shall for ever hereafter be a member of, and in Communion with the Church of England. as by Law established; And that the Governors of the said College, and their successors, for ever, shall be one body Corporate and politick, in deed, fact, and name, and shall be called, named, and distinguished, by the name of the Governors of the College of the Province of New York, in the City of New York, in America, and them and their successors, by the name of the Governors of the College of the Province of New York, in the City of New York, in America, one Body Corporate and politick, in deed, fact, and name, really and fully, we do for us, our heirs and Successors, Erect, Ordain, make, Constitute, declare, and Create by these presents, and that by that name, they shall and may have perpetual succession: *And* we do for us, our heirs, and successors, for the Continuance and Better Establishment of the said College, Will, Give, Grant, Ordain, Constitute, and appoint, that in the said

College, to be Erected and Built upon the Lands aforesaid there shall from henceforth forever be a Body Corporate and politick, Consisting of the Governors of the College of the Province of New York, in the City of New York, in America; And for the more full and perfect Erection of the said Corporation and Body politick, consisting of the Governors of the College of the Province of New York, in the City of New York, in America, we do will, Grant, ordain, Constitute, assign, Limitt, and appoint, by these presents, the most Reverend Father in God, our Trusty and well beloved *Thomas*, Lord Archbishop of Canterbury, and the most Reverend the Lord Archbishop of Canterbury for the time being; The Right Honorable Dunk, Earl of Halifax, first Lord Commissioner for Trade and Plantations, and the first Lord Commissioner for Trade and plantations for the time being; Our now Lieutenant Governor and Commander in chief of our said Province of New York, and the Governor or Commander in chief of our said Province for the time being; the eldest Councilor of our said Province now and for the time being; the Judges of our Supreme Court of Judicature of our said Province now and for the time being; the Secretary of our said Province now and for the time being; the Attorney General of our said Province now and for the time being; the Speaker of the General Assembly of our said Province now and for the time being; the Treasurer of our said Province now and for the time being; the Mayor of our City of New York in our said Province now and for the time being; the Rector of Trinity Church in our said City of New York now and for the time being; the Senior Minister of the Reformed Protestant Dutch Church in our said City now and for the time being; the

Minister of the ancient Lutheran Church in our said City now and for the time being; the Minister of the French Church in our said City now and for the time being; the Minister of the Presbeterian Congregation in our said City for the time being; the President of the said College, appointed by these Presents, and the President of the said College for the time being, to be chosen as herein after is directed, and twenty four other Persons, Who shall be called and named, and are hereby called and named, the Governors of the College of the Province of New York, in the City of *New York* in *America; And* for *that* purpose We have elected, nominated, ordained, constituted, limited, and appointed, and by these Presents do, for us, our Heirs, and Successors, elect, nominate, ordain, constitute, limit, and appoint, the said most Reverened Father in God, *Thomas*, Lord Archbishop of Canterbury, and the Lord Archbishop of Canterbury for the time being; The Right Honourable Dunk, Earl of Halifax, first Lord Commissioner for Trade and Plantations, and the first Lord Commissioner for Trade and Plantations for the time being; our now Lieutenant Governor and Commander in Chief of our Province of New York, and the Governor or Commander in chief of our said Province for the time being; the eldest Councilor of our said Province now and for the time being; the Judges of our Supreme Court of Judicature of our said Province now and for the time being; the Secretary of our said Province now and for the time being; the Attorney General of our said Province now and for the time being; the Speaker of the General Assembly of our said Province now and for the time being; the Treasurer of our said Province now and for the time being; the Mayor of our said City of New York now and for the time being; the Rector of Trinity Church in our said City now and for the time being; the Senior Minister of the Reformed Protestant Dutch Church in our said City now and for the time being; the Minister of the ancient Lutheran Church in our said City now and for the time being; the Minister of the French Church in our said City now and for the time being; the Minister of the Presbiterian Congregation in our said City for the time being; the President of the said College, appointed by these Presents, and the President of the said College for the time being; and Archibald Kennedy, Joseph Murray, Josiah Martin, Paul Richard, Henry Cruger, William Walton, John Watts, Henry Beekman, Philip Ver Planck, Frederick Philipse, Joseph Robinson, John Cruger, Oliver De Lancey, James Livingston, Esquires, Benjamin Nicoll, William Livingston, Joseph Read, Nathaniel Marston, Joseph Haynes, John Livingston, Abraham Lodge, David Clarkson, Leonard Lispenard, and James De Lancey the Younger, Gentlemen, to be the present Governors of the said College; and we do by these Presents ordain and appoint our well beloved Samuel Johnson, Doctor of Divinity, to be the first and present President of the said College, for and during his Good Behaviour; and do will that he and the President for the time being after him, who shall also hold his office during Good behaviour, shall have the Immediate care of the Education and Government of the students that shall be sent to and admitted into the said College for Instruction and Education, according to such Rules and orders as shall be made by the Governors of the said College; *And* they are by these presents made and constituted a Body Corporate and politick, by the said name of the Governors of the College of the province of New York, in the City of New York, in America; and they and their successors, by the said name of the Governors of the College of the province of New York, in the City of New York, in America, be, and for ever hereafter shall be, a Body politick and Corporate, in deed, fact, and name, and shall be Capable and able in Law to sue and be sued, Implead and be Impleaded, answer and be Answered unto, Defend and be Defended, In all Courts and places, before Us, our Heirs and Successors, and before all and any the Judges, Justices, Officers, and Ministers of Us, our Heirs and Successors, in any Court or Courts, place and places Whatsoever, in all and all manner of actions, suits, Complaints, Pleas, causes, matters, and demands whatsoever, and of what kind or nature soever, in as full, ample manner and form as any of our other Liege Subjects of our said Province of New York can or may sue and be sued, Implead and be Impleaded, defend and be Defended, by any Lawfull ways and means whatsoever. *And, also,* that they and their successors, by the said name of the Governors of the College of the Province of New York, in the City of New York, in America, be, and for ever hereafter, shall be a Body Corporate, Capable and able in Law to purchase, take, hold, receive, Enjoy, and have any messuages, houses, Lands, Tenements, and Hereditaments, and real Estate whatsoever, in Fee simple, or for Term of Life, or Lives, or Years, or in any other manner howsoever, for the use of the said College; *Provided always,* the clear yearly value thereof do not exceed the sum of Two Thousand pounds Sterling; and also Goods, Chattells, Books, moneys, annuities, and all other things of what nature and kind soever. And, also, that they and their Successors, by the same name of the Governours of the College of the

Province of New York, in the City of New York, in America, to and for the use of the said College, shall and may have full power and authority to Erect and build any house or houses, or other Buildings, as they shall think necessary or convenient; and also to Give, Grant, Bargain, sell, demise, assign, or otherwise dispose of all or any messuages, Lands, Tenements, Rents, and other Hereditaments, and real Estate, and all Goods, Chattells, money, and other things whatsoever, as to them shall seem fitt, either in the payment of the Salary or Salaries of the President, Fellows, and Professors of the said College, or any other Officers or ministers of the same, at their will and pleasure: excepting always, and it is, *Nevertheless*, our True Intent and meaning that the said Governors of the said College for the time being, and their Successors, or any of them, shall not do or suffer to be done, at any time hereafter, any act or thing whereby or by means whereof the Lands set apart and offered to be Conveyed by the Rector and Inhabitants of the City of New York, In Communion of the Church of England as by Law Established, for the use of the College, or any part thereof, shall be Vested, Conveyed, or Transferred, to any other person, contrary to the true meaning hereof, other than by such Leases as are hereafter mentioned: our will and pleasure is, therefore, and we do for us our heirs and Successors will and ordain, that no Grant or Lease of the said Land, or any part thereof, shall be made by the said Governors of the said College which shall exceed the number of Twenty one Years, and That either in possession or not above three years before the End and Expiration or Determination of the Estate or Estates in possession. *And* we do by these presents will, ordain, and direct, that the said Governors of the said College (Except always the Lord Archbishop of Canterbury for the time being, and our first Lord Commissioner for Trade and Plantations) do, at their first meeting, after the receipt of these our Letters patents, and before they proceed to any business of and concerning the said College, take the oaths appointed to be taken by an act passed in the first year of our Late Royal Father's Reign, Entituled, [an Act for the further security of his Majesty's Person and Government, and the Succession of the Crown, in the Heirs of the late Princess Sophia, being protestants, and for extinguishing the Hopes of the pretended Prince of wales, and his open and Secret abettors,] and make and subscribe the declaration mentioned in An Act of Parliament made in the twenty fifth year of the Reign of King Charles the second, Entituled, [an act for preventing Dangers which may happen from popish Recusants;] *As also*, an oath, faithfully to execute the trust Reposed in them, as members of the said Corporation, which Oaths we authorize and Impower the Justices of our Supreme Court of Judicature, for our said Province of New York for the time being, any or either of them to administer; and that when, and as often as any person or persons, either by his office or place in our said Government, or Elsewhere, (Except always the Lord Archbishop of Canterbury for the time being, and our first Lord Commissioner for Trade and Plantations for the time being,) or by Choice of the said Governors of the said College, shall become, or be Chosen a Member or members of the said Corporation, they shall, before they are admitted, or enter into the said office or Trust, take the said Oaths, and Subscribe the said Declaration to be administered to them in the manner above directed. *And* we do further will, ordain, and direct, that the Governors of the said College, shall yearly, and every year hereafter, forever, on the Second Tuesday in the Month of May, in every year, meet together in our said City of New York, for the Better taking care of, and Promoting the Interest of the said College; and that the said Governors of the said College, or any fifteen or more of them being met, shall be a Legal meeting of the said Corporation, and they, or the major part of them so met, shall have full power and authority to adjourn from day to day, as the Business of the said College may require, and to do, execute, and perform all and every act and acts, thing and things whatsoever, which the said Governors of the said College are, or shall by these, our Letters patent, be authorized and Impowered to do, act, or Transact, in as full and ample manner, as if all and every of the members of the said Corporation were present. *And* we do will, ordain, and direct, that as our Right Trusty and well beloved Thomas, Lord Archbishop of Canterbury, and the Lord Archbishop of Canterbury for the time being; and our said first Lord Commissioner for Trade and Plantations, and the First Lord Commissioner for Trade and plantations for the time being, cannot attend the meetings of the said Corporation, they and each of them shall, from time to time, have full power and authority to appoint a Proxy, in writing, under their hand and seal, which person or persons so appointed by them, and each of them shall and may Represent them, and each of them, Respectively, according to such appointment, and shall have full power to vote and act as a Governor or Governors of the said Corporation, at any and every meeting of the said Corporation, as fully and amply as if they, the Constituents, and each of them were present at every such meeting or meetings ; *And, in Case* any other meeting or meetings of the said Governors of the said College shall, at any other time or times, be Judged and deemed Necessary for the Carrying on and promoting of the Business and Interest of the said College, or the Government thereof, by any five members of the said Corporation, we do, by these presents, authorize and Impower such five members by writing, and under their hands, to direct the Clerk of the said Corporation to Give notice of the day appointed by them, for such meeting, at the said City of New York, by advertiseing the same in one or more of the publick news papers, at Least, seven Days before such meeting ; and, that at such meeting, the said Clerk, before entering on any Business, shall Certify such Notification under his hand, to the Board then met ; *Provided, always,* Fifteen or more of the said members shall be then met together, which said fifteen or more members, so met *In Pursuance* of such Notification, shall be a Legal meeting of the said Governors of the said College ; and they, or the major part of them so mett, shall have full power and authority to adjourn from day to day, as the Business of the said College may require, and to do, Transact, and perform, all matters and things whatsoever, that the said Governors of the said College are, or shall be authorized and Impowered to do, by these presents. *And of our further* Grace, Certain Knowledge, and meer motion, to the Intent that the said Corporation and Body politick, may answer the end of their erection and Constitution, and may have perpetual succession and Continue forever,

Wee do for us, our heirs, and Successors, Give and Grant unto the said Governors of the said College of the Province of New York, in the City of New York in America, and to their Successors for ever, that when and as often as they or any fifteen or more of the said members of the said Corporation or of their Successors shall be mett together at their said Yearly meeting herein before appointed, or at any other meeting upon Notification, as aforesaid, for the Service of the said College, that the Governor or Commander in chief of our said Province of New York, and, in his absence, the First person in Rank in our said Government, who holds his place as a Governor of the said Corporation by his office, place, or Dignity, and, in the absence of such, the Eldest Governor or member of the said Corporation then present, such Seniority to be taken according as they are named in this our Charter, during the lives of the present Governors and after their death, the Seniority to be taken and accounted as they have been a Longer or shorter time Governors of the said Corporation, shall preside at such meeting from time to time, and that at such meeting or meetings from time to time, they or the major part of them so met, shall have full power and authority to Elect, nominate, and appoint any person to be president of the said College in a Vacancy of the said Presidentship for and during his Good Behaviour; provided, always, such President Elect or to be elected by them, be a member of, and in Communion with the Church of England, as by Law Established; and, also, to Elect one or more Fellow or Fellows, Professor or Professors, Tutor or Tutors, to assist the President of the said College in the Education and Government of the Students belonging to the said College, which Fellow or

Fellows, Professor or Professors, Tutor or Tutors, and every of them, shall hold and Enjoy their said office or place, either at the will and pleasure of the Governors of the said Corporation or during his or their Good Behaviour, according as shall be agreed upon Between such Fellow or Fellows, Professor or Professors, Tutor or Tutors, and the said Governors of the said College, *Provided, always*, such Fellow or Fellows, Professor or Professors, Tutor or Tutors, before they or either of them enter into or Take upon themselves such office, do take the Oaths and subscribe the declaration hereinbefore directed, to be Taken and subscribed by the Governors of the said College before they enter upon their said Respective offices; and that when, and as often as any or either of the said offices shall become Vacant by death or otherwise, the said Governors, or the major part of any Fifteen or more of them so met as aforesaid, shall have full power to Elect, Nominate, and appoint, other or others in their places, upon the same proviso or Condition as aforesaid; and, *Also*, to Elect, Nominate, and appoint, upon the Death, Removal, Refusal to Qualify, or other vacancy of the place or places, of any Governor or Governors of the said Corporation not holding his office or place as a member of the same, by virtue of any other station, office, place, or dignity, from time to time, other or others in their places or stead as often as such vacancy shall happen, which Governor or Governors so from time to time elected and appointed, shall, by virtue of these presents, and of such Election and appointment be vested with all the powers, authoritys, and priviledges, which any Governor of the said Corporation is hereby Invested with. *And, we do further*, of our especial Grace, certain Knowledge, and meer motion, for us, our heirs, and Successors, Grant and ordain that when and as often as the president of the said College, or any Fellow, Professor or Tutor holding his place during Good behaviour shall misdemean himself in his or their said offices, and thereupon a Complaint or Charge in writing of such misdemeanour shall be exhibited against him or them by any member of the said Corporation, at any meeting or meetings of the said Corporation met and convened as aforesaid, That it shall be Lawful for the said members of the said Corporation then met, or the major part of them from time to time, upon Examination and due proof, to suspend or discharge such President, Fellow, Professor, or Tutor, from his said office, and other or others in his or their place or places to appoint; and, we do further for us, our heirs, and Successors, will and Grant that the said Governors of the said College, or the major part of any fifteen or more of them Convened and mett as aforesaid, shall and may, from time to time, as occasion may require, Elect, Constitute, and appoint, a Treasurer, Clerk, and Steward, for the said College, and to appoint them and each of them their respective Business and Trusts, and to displace and discharge from the Service of the said College such Treasurer, Clerk, or steward, and to elect other or others in their places and stead; and such Treasurer, Clerk, and steward, so Elected and appointed, we do for us, our heirs, and Successors, by these presents Constitute and Establish in their several offices, and do Give them full power and authority to Exercise the same in the said College, according to the direction and during the pleasure of the said Governors of the said College, or the major part of any fifteen or more of them Convened as aforesaid, as fully and freely as any other the like officers in any of our universities or any ot our Colleges in that part of our Kingdom of Great Britain called England, Lawfully may and ought to do: and we do further, of our Especial Grace, Certain Knowledge, and meer motion, Give and Grant unto the said Governors of the said College, that they and their Successors, or the major part of any fifteen or more of them Convened and mett Together in manner aforesaid, shall and may direct and appoint what Books shall be publickly read and taught in the said College, by the President, Fellows, Professors, and Tutors; and shall and may, under their Common seal, make and set down, and they are hereby fully Impowered, from time to time, to make and set down in writing, such Laws, ordinances, and orders, for the Better Government of the said College, and Students and Ministers thereof, as they shall think best for the General Good of the same, so that they are not Repugnant to the Laws and statutes of that part of our Kingdom of Great Britain called England, or of our said Province of New York, and do not extend to exclude any person of any Religious Denomination whatever from Equal Liberty and advantage of Education, or from any the Degrees, Liberties, Priviledges, Benefits, or Immunities of the said College, on account of his particular Tenets in matters of Religion; *And* such laws, Ordinances, and orders, which shall be so made as aforesaid, we do by these Presents, for us, our heirs, and Successors, Ratify, Confirm, and allow, as Good and Effectual to bind and oblige all and every the Students and Officers and Ministers of the said College; and we do hereby authorize and Impower the said Governors of the said College, or the major part of any fifteen or more of them, at any of their meetings

Convened as aforesaid, and the President, Fellows, and Professors for the time being, to put such Laws, ordinances, and orders, in execution, that is to say, such as Inflict upon any Student the Greater Punishments of Expulsion, Suspension, Degradation, and public Confession, by the Governors of the said College, or the major part of any fifteen or more of them, convened and met Together as aforesaid only; and such as Inflict the Lesser Punishments, by the President, Fellows, and Professors, or any of them, according to the true Intent of such Laws, ordinances, and orders, as shall be made In Pursuance of these presents for that purpose. *And* we do further will, ordain, and direct, that there shall be forever hereafter Publick morning and evening service Constantly performed in the said College, morning and evening for ever, by the President, Fellows, Professors, or Tutors, of the said College, or one of them, according to the Liturgy of the Church of England as by Law Established, or such a Collection of prayers out of the said Liturgy, with a Collect peculiar for the said College, as shall be approved of from time to time by the Governors of the said College, or the major part of any fifteen or more of them Convened as aforesaid: and we do further will and Grant, that the said Governors of the said College for the time being, or the major part of any fifteen or more of them Convened as aforesaid, shall have full power and Lawful authority to visit, order, punish, place, and displace, The Treasurer, Clerk, Steward, students, and other officers and ministers of the said College, and to order, Reform, and Redress, all and any the disorders, misdemeanors and abuses in the persons aforesaid, or any of them, and to Censure, suspend, or deprive them, or any or either of them, *So always*, that no visitation, act, or thing, in or Concerning the said College, be made or done by any other person or persons whatsoever but as is herein before Directed and Declared. *And* we do further, of our Especial Grace, Certain Knowledge, and meer motion, will, Give, and Grant, unto the said Governors of the said College, that for the Encouragement of the Students of the said College to Dilligence and Industry in their Studies, that they and their Successors, and the major part of any fifteen or more of them Convened and mett together as aforesaid, do, by the President of the said College, or any other person or persons by them authorized and appointed, Give and Grant any such degree and degrees to any the students of the said College, or any other person or persons by them thought worthy thereof, as are usually Granted by any or either of our universities or Colleges in that part of our Kingdom of Great Britain called England, and that the President, or such other persons to be appointed for that purpose as aforesaid, do sign and seal Diplomas or Certificates of such Degree or Degrees, to be kept by the Graduates as a Testimonial thereof. And *Further, of* our Especial Grace, Certain Knowledge, and meer motion, we do for us, our heirs, and Successors, will, Give, and Grant, *unto the said Governors of the said College*, and to their Successors, that they shall and may have one Common Seal, under which they shall and may pass all Grants, Diplomas, and all other writings whatsoever, requisite, necessary, or Convenient to pass under the seal of the said Corporation ; which seal shall be Engraven in such form and with such Devices and Inscriptions as shall be agreed upon by the said Governors of the said College, or the major part of any fifteen or more of them that shall be

Convened for the service of the said College, in the manner above directed ; and by these our Letters patent it shall and may be Lawful for them and their Successors, at any of their meetings Convened as aforesaid, as they shall see cause, to Break, Change, alter and new make the same, or any other common Seal, when and as often as to them shall seem convenient. *And we*, further, for us, our heirs, and Successors, Give and Grant unto the said Governors of the said College, and their Successors, or the major part of any fifteen or more of them Convened as aforesaid, full power and authority, from time to time, and at all times hereafter, to nominate and appoint all other Inferior officers or Ministers which they shall think convenient and necessary for the use of the College, not herein particularly named or mentioned, which Officers and Ministers we do hereby Impower to execute their Respective offices or Trusts, during the will and pleasure only of the Governors of the said College, or the major part of any fifteen or more of them Convened as aforesaid, as fully and freely as any other the like Officers or ministers in and of our Universities or any other College in that part of our Kingdom of Great Britain Called England may or ought to do. *And, Lastly*, of our Express will and pleasure, and meer motion, we do, for us, our heirs, and Successors, Give and Grant unto the said Governors of the said College, and to their Successors for ever, that these our Letters patent, being entered of Record, as is hereinafter particularly Expressed, or the Enrollment thereof, shall be Good and Effectual in the Law, to all Intents and purposes, against us, our heirs, and Successors, without any other Lycense, Grant, or Confirmation, from *us*, our heirs, or Successors, hereafter by the said Governors of the said College to be had or obtained, Notwithstanding the not reciting or misrecital, or not naming or misnaming of the aforesaid offices, Franchises, Priviledges, Immunities, or other the premises or any of them ; and notwithstanding a writt *ad Quod Damnum* hath not issued forth to inquire of or concerning the Premises, or any of them, before the ensealing hereof, any Statute, act, Ordinance, or provision or any other matter or thing to the Contrary thereof in any wise Notwithstanding ; *To have, hold, and Enjoy,* all and singular the Priviledges, Liberties, advantages, and Immunities, and all and singular other the Premises herein or hereby Granted, or meant, mentioned, or Intended to be herein and hereby Given and Granted unto them, the said Governors of the said College of the Province of New York, in the City of New York, in America, and to their Successors for ever. *In Testimony* whereof, we have caused these our Letters to be made patent, and the Great seal of our Province of New York to be hereunto affixed, and the same to be entered of Record in our Secretary's office of our said Province, in one of the Books of Patent there Remaining. *Witness* our Trusty and well beloved *James De Lancey, Esq.*, our Lieutenant Governor, and Commander in chief in and over our Province of New York, and the Territories depending thereon in *America,* in, by, and with the Advice and Consent of our Council of our said Province, this thirty first day of October. in the year of our Lord one thousand seven hundred and fifty four, and of our Reign the twenty eighth. The following Erasures and Interlineations appearing in these our Letters Patent. That is to say, in the first skin, Line four, the word [Law]. Line nineteen, these words, [by these our Letters Patent, that there be Erected and made] Interlined: line twenty one, [with] wrote on Eraisure: line twenty two, [Law] Interlined. In the second skin, line Twelve, [the] interlined, and [Younger] wrote on Eraisure. In the third skin, the First line, [and secret,] and in the sixth Line, [Administered] wrote partly on eraisure. In the twelfth line, [And the first Lord Commissioner for Trade and Plantations] Interlined. And in the fourth skin, and first line, the word [*And*] Interlined.——————————————

——————————————CLARKE, Junior.

ACTS OF THE LEGISLATURE,

RELATING TO

COLUMBIA COLLEGE.

An ACT *to institute an University within this State, and for other Purposes therein mentioned.*

Passed April 13th, 1787. [Sess. 10. ch. 82. sec. 8, 9, 10, 11. Greenleaf's Edit. vol. i. p. 437. Kent & Radcliff's Edit. vol. ii. p. 336.]

VIII. *And be it further enacted by the authority aforesaid,* That the charter heretofore granted to the governors of the college of the province of New York, in the city of New York, in America, dated the thirty-first day of October, in the year of our Lord one thousand seven hundred and fifty-four, shall be, and hereby is fully and absolutely ratified and confirmed in all respects, except that the college thereby established, shall be henceforth called Columbia college: That the style of the said corporation shall be, The trustees of Columbia college, in the city of New York; and that no person shall be trustees of the same, in virtue of any offices, characters, or descriptions whatever; excepting also such clauses thereof as require the taking of oaths, and subscribing the declaration therein mentioned; and which render a person ineligible to the office of president of the college, on account of his religious tenets, and prescribe a form of public prayer to be used in the said college; and also excepting the clause thereof which provides, that the by-laws and ordinances to be made in pursuance thereof, should not be repugnant to the laws and statutes of that part of the kingdom of Great-Britain, called England; except also, that in all cases where fifteen governors are required to constitute a quorum for the despatch of business, thirteen trustees shall be sufficient. Provided always, That the by-laws and ordinances to be made by the trustees of the said Columbia college, shall not be contrary to the constitution and laws of this state.

IX. *And be it further enacted by the authority aforesaid,* That James Duane, Samuel Provost, John H. Livingston, Richard Varick, Alexander Hamilton, John Mason, James Wilson, John Gano, Brockholst Livingston, Robert Harpur, John Daniel Gross, Johann Christoff Kunze, Walter Livingston, Lewis A. Scott, Joseph Delaplaine, Leonard Lispenard, Abraham Beach, John Lawrence, John Rutherford, Morgan Lewis, John Cochran, Gershom Seixas, Charles M'Knight, Thomas Jones, Malachi Treat, Samuel Bard, Nicholas Romein, Benjamin Kissam, and Ebenezer Crossby, shall be, and they are hereby constituted and declared to be the present trustees of Columbia college, in the city of New York, and that when by the death or resignation, or removal of any of the said trustees, the number of those trustees shall be reduced to twenty-four, then and from thenceforth the said twenty-four trustees shall be, and they hereby are declared and constituted trustees of the said Columbia college, in perpetual succession, according to the true intent and meaning of the said charter; and all vacancies thereafter shall be supplied in the manner thereby directed.

X. *And be it further enacted by the authority aforesaid,* That all and singular the power, authority, rights, privileges, franchises, and immunities, so heretofore granted to, and vested in the said governors of the college of the province of New-York, in the city of New-York, in America, by the said charter, excepting as before excepted, shall be, and the same hereby are granted to and vested in the trustees of Columbia college, in the city of New-York, and their successors forever, as fully and effectually, to all intents and purposes, as if the same were herein particularly specified and expressed; and all and singular the lands, tenements, hereditaments, and real estate, goods, chattels, rents, annuities, moneys, books, and other property, whereof the said governors of the college of the province of New-York, in the city of New-York, in America, were seised, possessed, or entitled, under and in virtue of the said charter, or with which the regents of the said university were invested, under or by virtue of the said acts, for the use or benefit of the said Columbia college, shall be, and the same hereby are granted to and vested in the said trustees of Columbia college, in the city of New-York, and their successors forever, for the sole use and benefit of the said college; and it shall and may be lawful to and for the said trustees and their successors, to grant, bargain, sell, demise, improve, and dispose of the same, as to them shall seem meet. Provided always, That the lands given and granted to the governors of the college of the province of New-York, in the city of New-York, in America, by the corporation, heretofore styled, The rector and inhabitants of the city of New-York, in communion of the church of England, as by law established, on part whereof the said college is erected, shall not be granted for any greater estate, or in any other manner, than is limited by the said charter.

XI. *And be it further enacted by the authority aforesaid,* That when any special meeting of the trustees of the said college shall be deemed necessary, it shall and may be lawful to and for the senior trustee of the said college, then in the city of New-York, and taking upon himself the exercise of the office, (which seniority shall be determined according to the order in which the said trustees are named in this act, and shall be elected hereafter,) and he is hereby authorized and required, on application for that purpose in writing under the hands of any five or more of the said trustees, to appoint a time for such special meeting, in some convenient place within the said city, and to cause due notice thereof to be given in the manner directed by the said charter.

XXII. *And be it further enacted by the authority aforesaid,* That the act, entitled, An act for granting certain privileges to the college heretofore called King's college, for altering the name and charter thereof, and erecting an university within this state, passed the 1st day of May, 1784; and the act, entitled, An act to amend an act, entitled, An act for granting certain privileges to the college heretofore called King's college, for altering the name and charter thereof, and erecting an university within this state, passed the 26th day of November, 1784, be, and they are hereby severally repealed.

[The 8th, 9th, 10th & 11th §§ of the preceding Act repealed by § 10, act March 23, 1810, following.]

An ACT *to encourage Literature, by Donations to Columbia College, and to the several Academies in the State.*

Passed April 11th, 1792. [Sess. 15. ch. 69. sec. 1. 3. Greenleaf's Edit. vol. ii. p. 479.]

WHEREAS it has been represented to the legislature, that the funds of Columbia college, in this state, have, in consequence of events which took place during the late war, been so far diminished, as to render it impracticable for the trustees to defray certain necessary expenses which have accrued to the college, in consequence of the alterations in the streets of the city of New York, and to repair the losses which the college sustained during the late war, with respect to its library, and to incur such further expenses as would render the seminary more extensively useful, without pecuniary aid from the legislature: For remedy whereof,

I. *Be it enacted by the People of the State of New York, represented in Senate and Assembly,* That there shall be allowed and paid to the trustees of Columbia college, or their order, for the use of the institution, the sum of fifteen hundred pounds, for the purpose of enlarging its library, and the sum of two hundred pounds for a chemical apparatus; and the sum of twelve hundred pounds for the purpose of building a wall, necessary to support the grounds of the college, and the further sum of five thousand pounds for the purpose of erecting a hall and an additional wing to the college, pursuant to the original plan of the institution; and the treasurer is hereby authorized to pay the said respective sums out of such moneys as may be or may come into the treasury, of the annual revenue of the state, and which may not be appropriated for the purpose of supporting government, or satisfying claims against the state, or for completing the sum of two hundred thousand pounds to be loaned in the several counties of this state, by virtue of the act, entitled, "An act for loaning moneys belonging to the state."

III. *And be it further enacted,* That the treasurer shall annually, for five years, unless otherwise directed by the legislature, pay to the trustees of Columbia college, or their order, out of the like moneys as above described, the sum of seven hundred and fifty pounds, to be applied to the payment of the salaries of such additional professors in the said college, as the said trustees shall think proper to appoint.

[After the expiration of the five years, the payment of the sum of seven hundred and fifty pounds was continued for the further term of two years by an act, entitled, "An act for the payment of certain officers of government and other contingent expences." Passed April 11, 1796.—(3 *Greenleaf* 340.)]

In an act, entitled, "An act respecting Union college, and for the purposes therein mentioned," passed March 30th, 1797, the following clause occurs:

And be it further enacted, that the treasurer of this state, shall annually, on the first Tuesday of July, in every year hereafter, during the pleasure of the legislature, pay to the trustees of Columbia college, the sum of five hundred dollars, to be appropriated by the said trustees to the preservation of the Anatomical Museum in the said college, and for procuring additional articles thereto, and for making such allowance as they shall judge proper to the professor of Anatomy in said college, for his services in the care and charge of such museum.—(3 *Greenleaf* 449.)

An ACT *to amend the Act entitled, "An Act for the Encouragement of Literature."*

Passed April 3d, 1802. [Sess. 25. ch. 105. sec. 1, 2. Webster's Edit. vol. iii. p. 165.]

WHEREAS it appears, from a report of the surveyor-general, that the grant of a certain tract of land in the county of Washington, adjoining the south end of Lake George, to the regents of the university, in and by the act, entitled, "An act for the further encouragement of literature," interferes with the bounds of lands previously granted; and the regents having prayed for a grant of other lands adjoining the same, and in lieu thereof, to enable them the more effectually to fulfill the purposes for which the grant of those lands was intended: Therefore,

I. *Be it enacted by the People of the State of New-York, represented in Senate and Assembly*, That the said regents of the university, and their successors, shall be and hereby are vested with the seisin and possession of the lands hereafter described, belonging to the people of this state; that is to say, a certain tract of land in the county of Washington, adjoining the south end of Lake George, beginning on the east shore of the said lake, where the westerly bounds of a tract of two thousand acres, granted by letters patent to William Houghton, strikes the same, and running thence along the said Houghton's tract southerly and westerly to the northwest corner thereof, then with a straight line to the most westerly corner of a tract of two hundred acres granted by letters patent to John Jones, then along the southerly bounds thereof, to Lake George, and then along the same southerly, easterly, and northerly, to the place of beginning, containing one thousand seven hundred and twenty-four acres of land; and the former grant to the said regents, so far as the same included lands not herein described, shall be void.

II. *And be it further enacted,* That it shall be lawful for the said regents to grant and convey to the trustees of Columbia and Union colleges, and their successors, the lands above described, together with the lands at Ticonderoga and Crown Point already vested in the said regents, in such proportions as they shall deem just and reasonable, for the use of the said colleges respectively.

An ACT *relative to Columbia College in the City of New York.*

Passed March 23d, 1810. [Sess. 33. ch. 85. Webster & Skinner's Edit. of Statutes, vol. vi. p. 24.]

WHEREAS the trustees of Columbia college, in the city of New-York, have represented, that sundry impediments to their trust, and to the interest of literature in the college, are found by experience from certain restrictions and defects in their charter, and have prayed relief, and that their charter, when amended, may be comprised in one act: Therefore,

I. BE *it enacted by the people of the State of New York, represented in Senate and Assembly,* That John H. Livingston, Richard Varick, Brockholst Livingston, Abraham Beach, John Lawrence, Gershom Seixas, Richard Harison, John Watts, William Moore, Cornelius I. Bogart, John M. Mason, Edward Dunscomb, George C. Anthon, John N. Abeel, James Tillary, John H. Hobart, Benjamin Moore, Egbert Benson, Gouverneur Morris, Jacob Radcliff, Rufus King, Samuel Miller, Oliver Wolcott, and John B. Romeyn, the present trustees of the said college, and their successors, shall be and remain forever hereafter, a body politic and corporate, in fact and in name, by the name of "The trustees of Columbia College, in the city of New York," and by that name shall and may have continual succession for ever hereafter, and shall be able in law to sue and be sued, implead and be impleaded, answer and be answered unto, defend and be defended, in all courts and places whatsoever, and may have a common seal, and may change and alter the same at their pleasure, and also, shall be able in law to take by purchase, gift, grant, devise, or in any other manner, and to hold any real and personal estate whatsoever; *Provided always*, The clear yearly value of the real estate to be so acquired, shall not exceed the sum of twenty thousand dollars; and also that they and their successors shall have power to give, grant, bargain, sell, demise, or otherwise dispose of, all or any part of the said real and personal estate, as to them shall seem best for the interest of the said college.

II. *And be it further enacted*, That the said trustees, and their successors, shall forever hereafter have full power and authority to direct and prescribe the course of study, and the discipline to be observed in the said college, and also to select and appoint by ballot or otherwise, a president of the said college, who shall hold his office during good behaviour; and such professor or professors, tutor or tutors, to assist the president in the government and education of the students belonging to the said college, and such other officer or officers, as to the said trustees shall seem meet, all of whom shall hold their offices during the pleasure of the trustees: *Provided always*,

That no such professor, tutor, or other assistant officer shall be trustee.

III. *And be it further enacted*, That if complaint shall be made in writing to the said trustees, or their successors, by any member of the said corporation of any misbehaviour in office by the president, it shall be lawful for the said trustees, or their successors, from time to time, upon examination, and such due proof of misbehaviour, to suspend or discharge such president, and to appoint another in his place.

IV. *And be it further enacted*, That eleven of the said trustees, lawfully convened, as is hereinafter directed, shall be a quorum for the dispatch of all business, except for the disposal of real estate, or for the choice or removal of a president, for either of which purposes there shall be a meeting of at least thirteen trustees.

V. *And be it further enacted*, That the said trustees shall have full power and authority to elect by ballot their own chairman once in every year, or at such other periods as they shall prefer.

VI. *And be it further enacted*, That the said trustees shall also have power, by a majority of votes of the members present, to elect and appoint, upon the death, removal out of the state, or other vacancy of the place or places of any trustee or trustees, other or others, in his or their places or stead as often as such vacancy shall happen; and also to make and declare vacant the seat of any trustee who shall absent himself from five successive meetings of the board; and also to meet upon their own adjournment, and so often as they shall be summoned by their chairman, or in his absence by the senior trustee; whose seniority shall be accounted according to the order in which the said trustees are named in this act, and shall be elected hereafter; *Provided always*, That the said chairman or senior trustee shall not summon a meeting of the corporation unless required thereto in writing by three of the members; *And provided also*, That he cause notice of the time and place of the said meeting to be given in one or more of the public newspapers printed in the City of New York, at least three days before such meeting: and that every member of the corporation resident in the city shall be previously advertised in writing of the time and place of every such meeting.

VII. *And be it further enacted*, That the said trustees and their successors, shall have power and authority to grant all such literary honours and degrees, as are usually granted by any university, college, or seminary of learning in this state, or in the United States; and in testimony of such grant to give suitable diplomas under their seal, and the signatures of the president and such professors, or tutors of the college, as they shall judge expedient; which diplomas shall entitle the possessors respectively to all the immunities and privileges which either by usage or statute are allowed to possessors of similar diplomas from any university, college, or seminary of learning.

VIII. *And be it further enacted*, That the said trustees and their successors shall have full power and authority to make all ordinances and by-laws which to them shall seem expedient for carrying into effect the designs of their institution; *Provided always*, That such ordinance or by-laws shall not make the religious tenets of any person a condition of admission to any privilege or office in th said college, nor be inconsistent with the constitution and laws of this state, nor with the constitution and laws of the United States.

IX. *And be it further enacted,* That all the real and personal estate whatsoever and wheresoever, which were formerly vested in the governors of the college of the province of New-York, in the city of New-York, in America, or in the trustees of Columbia college in the city of New-York, be and the same is hereby confirmed to and vested in the said trustees of Columbia college in the city of New-York, and their successors for ever, for the sole use and benefit of the said college; and that it shall and may be lawful to and for the said trustees, and their successors, to grant, bargain, sell, demise, improved and dispose of the same, as to them shall seem meet; *Provided always,* that the lands given and granted to the governors of the college of the province of New-York, in the city of New-York, in America, by the corporation heretofore styled "The Rector and Inhabitants of the city of New-York, in communion of the Church of England, as by law established," on part whereof the said college is erected, shall not be granted for any greater term of time than sixty-three years.*

X. *And be it further enacted,* That the eighth, ninth, tenth, and eleventh sections of the act entitled, "an act to institute an university within this state, and for other purposes therein mentioned," passed the thirteenth day of

---

*See Act, passed April 15, 1852, *post.*

April, in the year of our Lord one thousand seven hundred an eighty-seven, be and the same are hereby repealed.*

An ACT *to render the Provost of Columbia College in the city of New-York, eligible to be a trustee thereof.*

Passsed Feb. 14th, 1812. [Sess. 35. ch. 6. Webster & Skinner's Edit. vol. vi. p. 348.]

Whereas the trustees of Columbia college have, by their petition, prayed that the provost of the said college may be made eligible as a trustee of said college:

Be it enacted by the People of the State of New York, represented in Senate and Assembly, That it shall and may be lawful for the provost of Columbia college, in the city of New York, for the time being, to be elected and act as a trustee of the said college, anything contained in the act entitled, "an act relative to Columbia college in the city of New York," or in any other act or charter of the said college, to the contrary notwithstanding.

An ACT *instituting a Lottery for the promotion of Literature, and for other purposes.*

Passed April 13th, 1814. [Sess. 37. ch. 120, sec. 6, 7, Webster & Skinner's Edit. vol. iii. p. 142.]

VI. *And be it further enacted,* That all the right, title, and interest of the people of this state in and to all that certain piece or parcel of land, with the appurtenances, situate in the ninth ward of the city of New York, known by

*See also the Act passed April 9, 1813, sess. 36 ch. 82., Van Ness & Woodworth, vol. ii. p. 265, and *new Revised Statutes*, vol. iii. p. 236, re-enacting the above act, omitting only the Preamble, and the names of Trustees: and with the additional proviso, as to the eligibility of the Provost as a Trustee.

the name of the Botanic Garden, and lately conveyed to the people of this state by David Hosack, with the appurtenances, be and the same is hereby granted to and vested in the trustees of Columbia college, in the city of New York, their successors and assigns; but this grant is made upon the express condition, that the college establishment shall be removed to the said tract of land hereby granted, or to lands adjacent thereto, within twelve years from this time; and if the said establishment shall not be so removed within the time above limited, then and from thenceforth, this grant shall cease and be void, and the premises hereby granted shall thereupon revert to the people of this state.

VII. *And be it further enacted,* That the trustees of Columbia college shall, within three months from the time of the passage of this act, transmit to the trustees of each of the other colleges in this state, a list of the different kinds of plants, flowers, and shrubs in said garden; and within one year thereafter, the said trustees of Columbia college, shall deliver at the said garden, if required, at least one healthy exotic flower, shrub, or plant of each kind, of which they shall have more than one at the time of application, together with the jar or vessel containing the same, to the trustees of each of the other colleges of this state, who shall apply therefor.

An ACT *relative to Columbia College, in the city of New York.*

Passed February 19th, 1819. [Sess. 42. ch. 19. Gould & Co's Edit. vol. v. p. 26.]

WHEREAS it is of the first importance in a free state, that seminaries of learning should be carefully protected, and, from time to time, receive the fostering aid of the legislature: *And whereas,* with these views, all the right, title, and interest of the people of this state in a certain piece or parcel of land, situate in the ninth ward of the city of New-York, called "The Botanic Garden," was in and by an act of the legislatuie, entitled "an act instituting a lottery for the promotion of literature, and for other purposes," passed April 13th, 1814, given and granted to Columbia College, subject to certain conditions therein specified: *And whereas* the said grant has not been productive of the benefits intended by the said act: Therefore,

I. *BE it enacted by the People of the State of New York, represented in Senate and Assembly,* That that part of the sixth section of the act, entitled, "an act instituting a lottery for the promotion of literature, and for other purposes," passed April 13th, 1814, which contains a condition to the grant made to the trustees of Columbia college, that the college establishment shall be removed to the tract of land thereby granted, or to the lands adjacent thereto, and the seventh section of the said act, be and the same are hereby repealed.

II. *And be it further enacted,* That the sum of ten thousand dollars be paid by the treasurer, on the warrant of the comptroller, to the trustees of Columbia College, out of any moneys not otherwise appropriated, to be applied by the said trustees as the interests of the saia college may require.

An ACT *to amend an act, entitled "An Act relative to Columbia College, in the city of New York," passed March* 23, 1810. *(Laws of* 1852, *ch.* 310.*)*

Passed April 15, 1852.

The People of the State of New York, represented in Senate and Assembly, do enact as follows:

I. The ninth section of the act entitled, "An act relative to Columbia college, in the city of New-York," passed March 23d, eighteen hundred and ten, is hereby amended, by adding at the end of said section the following words: "unless the consent of said grantors in writing, under their corporate seal, shall be first had and obtained to the disposal thereof, free from such restriction."

An ACT *to authorize the trustees of Columbia College in the city of New York, to take and hold certain real estate.* (*Laws of* 1857, *chap.* 132.)

Passed March 19, 1857, three-fifths being present.

The People of the State of New York, represented in Senate and Assembly, do enact as follows:

SECTION 1. The Trustees of Columbia college, in the city of New York, are hereby authorized to purchase and take, and to hold in fee simple, and dispose of a certain parcel of land situate in the nineteenth ward of the city of New York, and bounded northerly by the southerly side of Fiftieth street, southerly by the northerly side of Forty-ninth street, easterly by a line parallel with and one hundred feet distant westerly from the westerly side of the Fourth avenue, and westerly by a line parallel with and five hundred feet distant easterly from the easterly side of the Fifth avenue, or any part or parts thereof, and dispose of the proceeds for the use and purposes of said college.

§ 2. This act shall take effect immediately.

An ACT *to authorize the trustees of Columbia College, in the city of New York, to take and hold certain real estate. (Laws* 1860, *chap.* 51.*)*

Passed March 2, 1860.

The People of the State of New York, represented in Senate and Assembly, do enact as follows:

SECTION 1. The trustees of Columbia college, in the city of New York, are hereby authorized to purchase and take, and to hold in fee simple, and dispose of such land, in addition to that which they were authorized to take and hold under the act, entitled "An act to authorize the trustees of Columbia College, in the city of New York, to take and hold certain real estate," passed March nineteenth, eighteen hundred and fifty-seven, as shall be situated in the city of New York, and shall, together with the land taken and held under the said act, be comprehended within the following bounds, to wit: the southerly side of Fiftieth street; the westerly side of the Fourth avenue; the northerly side of Forty-ninth street, and a line drawn parallel with the Fourth avenue, and distant four hundred and fifty feet westerly therefrom, or any part or parts thereof.

An ACT *relative to the law school of Columbia College.*
(*Laws of* 1860, *chap.* 202.)

Passed April 7th, 1860.

The People of the State of New York, represented in Senate and Assembly, do enact as follows:

SECTION 1. The professors in the law school of Columbia college, and the law committee of the trustees of said college, viz.: Samuel B. Ruggles, Hamilton Fish, Alexander W. Bradford, Gouverneur M. Ogden, George T. Strong and William Betts, and such persons as shall from time to time form such law committee, any three of whom, being counselors at law, shall form a quorum upon whose examination and recommendation, as evidenced by the diploma of said college granted upon such recommendation, any graduate of said law school shall be admitted to practice as an attorney and counselor at law in all the courts of this state. No diploma shall be sufficient for such admission which is given for any period of attendance upon said law school for a less term than eighteen months, but this period of eighteen months shall not apply to the members of the present senior class in said law school who may be admitted to practice as aforesaid upon the examination and recommendation of said committee, and upon the evidence of the diploma of the college.

§ 2. All acts and parts of acts inconsistent with this act are hereby repealed.

§ 3. This act shall take effect immediately.

An ACT *in relation to Columbia College, in the city of New York. (Laws of* 1872, *chap.* 96.*)*

Passed March 8, 1872; three-fifths being present.

The People of the State of New York, represented in Senate and Assembly, do enact as follows:

SECTION 1. The trustees of Columbia College, in the city of New York, are hereby authorized, from time to time, to purchase and take and hold in fee simple, any lands situate in the city of New York, for a new site or sites for the said college or for any of the schools or necessary buildings of the same, and to sell and convey any lands now held by said college, but no lands owned by said college shall be exempt from taxation, except such as are or may be in actual use as a site or sites for said college.

§ 2. This act shall take effect immediately.

www.ingramcontent.com/pod-product-compliance
Lightning Source LLC
LaVergne TN
LVHW050513100826
845148LV00002B/317

* 9 7 8 1 4 2 5 5 2 1 7 8 3 *